BC

(...AND Y

MW01047637

BCZICAN

(...AND YOU CAN TOO...)

BY

BETH GRIFFIN

www.bookstandpublishing.com

Published by
Bookstand Publishing
Morgan Hill, CA 95037
3236_3

ISBN 978-1-58909-821-3

Printed in the United States of America

ACKNOWLEDGMENTS

Since I began writing this book, I became fascinated by the acknowledgments in other authors' books and surprised at their diversity. Now, since it's my turn I'll say it the best way I can.

My family has always been important to me and I want to thank my parents, Eugene and Naomi, for being strong-willed and purpose-driven for all seven of their children. A special thank you goes out to my sister, Terry, for not wavering when I didn't seem too enthralled about how to spend my Sundays. Still, she persevered. My other sisters, Robin and Leesa, and brothers, Tom, Brad and John all had a bearing in who I am today and I'm proud to have such incredible and interesting siblings. Each is intertwined in my story within the pages of this book. I want to acknowledge Master Photographer Beth Ann Sayles for the photo on the cover; my hairdresser and confidante, Louise "Lou" Robertson of Ladies and Gents Salon; and Evan Johnson for the superb cover design and layout as well as his computer expertise.

Thanks to Londa Briles Foster for sharing the way in my teenage years and introducing me to a healthy faith.

Thank you to Candis Cotter, an exceptional nurse that made me a better person, listened to my stories, and brought out the laughter for both of us.

Thanks to Mario Agosta, a special man who always believed in me and my effort to write . . . and finish this book.

Thank you, Dr. Phillip McGraw for the gift of your book, "Self Matters," which was the catalyst for this endeavor.

And thanks to Gavin de Becker, the author of "The Gift of Fear," a bearer of sound advice and a fascinating man. I appreciated that you allowed me to use quotes from your thought-provoking and valuable book.

I am indebted to all of you.

vi

INTRODUCTION

I was second born of seven children whose births would span over fifteen years. One older sister, two younger sisters, and three brothers were the mix. Our names in order were Terry, Beth, Robin, Tom, Leesa, Brad, and John. It had a kind of sing-song rhyme to it. We grew up in a cinder block home that my father, Eugene, built after leaving the Army and marrying his high school sweetheart and my mother, Naomi.

They chose to build in a portion of Waterford Township in Michigan, a relatively rural area at the time, with a beautiful lake less than seventy feet from our front door. Nothing was more pleasurable than canoeing in the spring, frolicking in the warm water mid-summer, learning to fish using a trusty bamboo pole, and waterskiing. Winter brought a lake covered in a sheet of ice and wishing for new ice skates for Christmas. There was always a way to spend the days after school and during summer and winter breaks.

There's an unusual scent in the air that lake water brings. In early spring, it smells fresh and clean and feels frigid to the touch. Easing into summer the scent changes and fills the air with the aroma of seaweed mixed with the faint gasoline and oil fumes from boats whizzing by. Tranquil sounds of playful water lapping the shore and softly splashing against the wooden dock were background music during sunsets and nighttime swims. Entertaining red wing black birds warbled their tune resembling the sound of the words "cong-a-lee" as they swayed back and forth perched atop cattails nearby. The neighborhood kids took their swimming lessons, played water tag, and participated in diving board antics each summer with us. We loved nature's playground that we called "our lake." The lake would be at the root of dreams to come; some nice and some not so nice.

Our house was the neighborhood hangout. There were always kids staying for lunch and sometimes dinner too. Our garage would become a spook house in the summer. Sometimes we'd publish a neighborhood newspaper. All of us played some musical instrument, so there was music in the house a great deal of the time. Growing up in a large family offered entertainment usually seen in good sitcoms and lots of responsibilities at an early age.

We looked out for one another. Our parents were good people and terrific role models.

I had my own thoughts about love. I was a "giver" and seemed to attract more "takers" in my life. Mom told me more than once that I was "too giving" and it was my "fatal flaw." I thought my needs were few. I wanted someone to love that would love me back – so simple yet so complex. It would turn out to be a huge undertaking directing me down confusing and sometimes dangerous paths.

People used to ask me why I felt the need to try so many new and different things. I once told my uncle, "I treat my life like a plate of hors d'oeuvres and I'd like to taste every single one on the plate." The real reason I've explored different careers, delved into new places to go, found different restaurants to try, and have enjoyed a plethora of interests is because I can. Anyone can if they want to bad enough

    . . . And that's why my car carries the following license plate: "BCZICAN."

Table of Contents

Acknowledgements v

Introduction vii

1. Brief Encounter 1
2. Lessons about Cruelty and Stealing 3
3. Attack Dogs and the Dinner Bell 5
4. Indoor Ice Rink: A Skater's Paradise 9
5. In Search of Dick Button 11
6. Cheerleading Was Nothing to Cheer About 13
7. Drowning in Flannel 15
8. Sewing Mania 19
9. Breasts and Barefoot on the Golf Course 21
10. A Fall Through the Ice and From Grace 23
11. Waterford Junior Miss She Was Not 25
12. A First Love Leaves for War 27
13. The Cobo Audition 33
14. Dear Jane, Sweet Jane 39
15. Coffee with Cops 43
16. Lessons and Practice in Love, Life, and Waitressing 47
17. Holiday on Ice Awaits and Waits 51
18. Hurts Abound as a Soldier Returns 57
19. Career Changes Needed 59
20. A Wedding to Remember 61
21. Major Missteps: The Corvette, The Burn, The Surprise 67
22. The Separation 75
23. The Doomsday Drink: The Hospital, The Earring and the
    Knife, The Visit 81
24. Real Estate School 89
25. Winning Two Trips, Keeping Half 91
26. Moving Out – The Piano Stays 95
27. The Suicide Scare 97
28. Super Bowl Sunday's Not So Super 101
29. Mental Incompetence 103
30. Grandma is My Roommate 105
31. Building Again 111
32. A Tumble and Near Tragedy 115
33. A Chance Meeting with Mom – Twice 119

34.	The Business/Marriage Mix	123
35.	A Strike to the Heart	127
36.	One Last Chance	131
37.	Moving on Up and Maybe to Beauty College	133
38.	The "Breakdown"	137
39.	I Love You, Goodbye	141
40.	Standing Ground, Lying Down, Nearly Drown	145
41.	A Nine Millimeter Rules	149
42.	Lawyers: Spread Sheets, Buy a Gun and Make a Will, Lipstick	151
43.	Beauty School Sanity and Laughter While Undercovers Wonder	155
44.	Despair Reigns	161
45.	Wanna Be a Model for a Day?	165
46.	Resumé for Jacqueline of All Trades	169
47.	The Blue Riviera	175
48.	Career Clatter	177
49.	A Handsome After-Work Surprise	181
50.	Another Try at Love	183
51.	Marriage, Moving On, and Moving Over	187
52.	Painful News for Graduation	189
53.	A Stunt Unavenged	197
54.	Emergency Trauma Time	199
55.	Drifting on Different Shifts	201
56.	Lakefront Move But No Boat	203
57.	Don't Touch	205
58.	Sandy the Psychologist	209
59.	Alone with a Piano in Tow	211
60.	Sparkling Eyes and Cowboy Boots	215
61.	New Digs	217
62.	Breaking the Boat	221
63.	Jail Work and Jealousy	227
64.	Gavin de Becker Was My Hero, Or: Stalker on a Bike, Switching Cars, In a Black Suit Wearing White Paint	231
65.	Bad Memories = Good Move	237
66.	Condo Heaven	239
Epilogue		241

Chapter 1

BRIEF ENCOUNTER

There was dead silence except for the pounding of my heart. When it was over, it was all I could do to sit on the edge of the bed trembling as I retraced the hem of my nightie. Over and over, I slid my fingers back and forth across the dark blue silky fabric. Hours passed. It was now 5:00 a.m. I hadn't been prepared for this long night, not even with a vivid imagination. But I was surprisingly calm, my face expressionless in the mirrored bedroom door facing me.

The tossing and turning started about 12:30 in the morning, then awakened me every thirty minutes or so. Last glance at the clock read 3:00 a.m. Why now on this night? It was 1999. At forty-nine I was single, alone, and having a fitful night's sleep. My work had been as unfulfilling as my relationships. Reluctantly, I rolled over placing my back to the door, and to the security motion detector monitor on the bedroom wall. Bad memories had made sleeping with my back to the door difficult. There was a sense of security seeing the solid red and green buttons lit. That meant all was well downstairs – my bonus for purchasing the model on this street of condominiums. The security alarm and detector were already installed when I moved in. Shortly after repositioning myself on my right side, I began to relax. A heavy sigh lingered as I exhaled. The edge of the bed I was so used to curling up on was empty now. Eyeing the time, I knew I would hate the annoying hum of the alarm clock in a few hours.

At 3:04 a.m. almost methodically, the edge of the mattress slowly began to descend, and an arm gently lay across me at the waist. What a comforting feeling, such an affectionate gesture, but suddenly my eyes popped open in utter disbelief. No one should be in this bedroom or sitting behind me on this bed. No one had a key to my home. My eyes quickly focused on a man's hand in front of my face. I didn't move a muscle frozen with fear. My heart was pounding so hard and fast, the sound filling my ears. Was he going to put his hand over my mouth? Hurt me? Smother me? Kill me?

In an instant, my plan was made. On a silent count of three, I would suddenly roll toward him as hard and fast as I could and knock him off the bed. Then, I'd run for my life. And I was glad I had worn something to bed. It's scary being vulnerable and naked. The rolling was swift and I leapt to my feet. But no one was on the floor. However, the glaring, yellow light on the motion detector was blinking frantically, letting me know there was movement downstairs. I hesitated at the top of the stairs until the blinking stopped. I wouldn't go down if he was still trying to escape. I would just let him leave. No slamming of doors, no glass breaking was heard. There it was – the dead silence. It made me more frightened.

Surging with adrenaline, I crept down the stairs turning on each light as I came to it. Suddenly, light was power. Not a thing out of place. The doors and windows were locked. One window was left to check – down in the pitch-black basement. I hesitated to grab a flashlight, and then nearly galloped down the basement steps taking two at a time, slapping each light switch upward as I passed. The window was untouched. I made my way back up the two flights of stairs, leaving all the lights on and feeling too foolish to call the police. No breaking and entering here. I sat on the edge of the bed until dawn attempting to figure out my brief encounter, envisioning that man's left hand, burning it into my memory and all the while stroking the hem of my gown, touching it ever so lightly with my fingertips. I had to think, but I needed to sleep. When I'm rested I told myself, I'll review things and it will make sense. There had to be a logical explanation. My life, however, had been anything but logical. And so began the mental journey of my life, recalling the pivotal moments from elementary school right up to this very night – a night that changed me.

Chapter 2

LESSONS ABOUT CRUELTY AND STEALING

A new elementary school, called Laura Smith Haviland opened and that was my new school for grades fourth, fifth, and sixth. The first year, girls pretty much stayed with girls on the playground while the boys played tag and kickball. However, while in the fifth grade, it became a mixture of both. There were times when some of the "rough" boys would pick on someone they singled out and chase them, throwing them down, humiliating them, sometimes hurting them. Other people would laugh especially if a person cried. It sickened me. One day, they turned to me and said, "It's your turn . . . you're it!" My classmates called me names, and picked up rocks and hurled them at me. Others joined in – even girls that I thought were my friends. These were neighborhood kids that rode my bus and played in my yard. They joined in, too. I was being struck in the head and the back – I was afraid. I tried to outrun them until I became trapped in a corner of the playground edged by anchor fencing. As I tried to climb the fence, my foot slipped underneath impaling my ankle on a sharp metal barb. My foot began bleeding drenching my sock and filling my shoe. I couldn't get loose. I was afraid to cry. I felt helpless. One of the girls became frightened and ran to find a teacher. She found Miss Hash, the fourth grade teacher who ran to the fence, telling everyone to "Get back!" in her southern twang, but soon she got very woozy from the blood. A maintenance man appeared and lifted a portion of fence up, releasing my tethered foot. I was sent home only to be taken for a tetanus shot. And on that day the meaning of friendships seemed completely distorted.

I did become friends later that summer with Marcia, a wonderful girl with a toothy grin, perfect teeth I might add, who lived about two miles from me. She was a tomboy as was I. We played softball on the same team, and rode our bikes all over the place. She lived a short distance from a farm owned by the Beutler's. It was early fall, their crops were mostly picked, and the apple trees hung heavy from the weight of a good yield. Mrs. Beutler grew Cortlands, one of the best eating apples ever when

3

picked while they're still tart. Marcia and I were on one of our bike trips when we passed the apple trees that day.

"Hey, I wonder if those apples taste as good as they look?" I asked. Marcia grinned. Soon, we had thrown down our bikes, and each picked a Cortland beauty and sat in the shade munching them down, relishing every bite. I was excited to have my brothers and sisters have a taste. Marcia had brothers and sisters, too. We laughed as we both pulled off our shoes and socks. Suddenly, socks became a practical container. Pretty soon, our white socks were bulging with apples. As we began to tie the socks to our handlebars, a voice boomed from behind us.

"Now, why would you two come and STEAL from me? All you had to do is ask me and I would have given you some. Instead you come and take what's not yours. Where did you learn that it's okay? Shame on you both!"

We were mortified. Slowly, we untied our socks, removed the stolen goods and handed them over to her while hanging our heads. Then she said something that surprised us both.

"I might need some help picking these next week, so come and see me so you can earn them the right way."

God love Mrs. Beutler. I never stole anything ever again. For years after, I would see her selling her apples and other crops at the Oakland County Farmers Market wearing a warm smile on that weathered face. That's where I bought my Cortlands.

Chapter 3

ATTACK DOGS AND THE DINNER BELL

Because of our growing family, getting everyone home each night for dinner was a chore for Mom until she was given "the dinner bell." This bell was large, loud, and clanged with authority. The sound would resonate for almost a mile. Because the lake was so close, the water carried its loud chime easily. My father mounted this bell on the upper corner of our house on the peak just above my parents' bedroom window. A clothesline was tied to it, and the rope was easily accessible by reaching through the open window. The younger kids in the family loved taking turns ringing the dinner bell over and over. My classmates would complain, "Geez, does your mother HAVE to ring that thing every night? My mom says I have to be home when the Griffin dinner bell rings!" So it went, echoing through family after family. We were considered an unpopular menace. But, we all knew that it meant, "Dinner in half an hour and you better be there." Mom was a stickler about us all eating together.

I was visiting a schoolmate I'll call Dina. I befriended her when I saw her sitting alone one day on the bus. She was a heavy-set girl with freckles and an only child. Her parents weren't together which I thought was sad. Her mother seemed to smoke a lot and there was usually a foggy haze in the house. She did have dogs – German Shepherds and Dobermans. We shared the same classroom in fourth through sixth grade. I spent the night at her house and was introduced to scrambled eggs with ketchup, interesting but no culinary delight. We only drowned our food in ketchup at home if it was something we couldn't stand, like lima beans or sauerkraut. It was a nice friendship until one day when the dinner bell rang.

I heard the clanging very clearly. It was fall and the air was so brisk I had worn a flannel shirt and jeans to her house. I said, "I have to go, Dina. There's the dinner bell."

"Well, I don't WANT you to go. I WANT you to stay! Stay here until my mom gets home from the store and then she can drive you home. She just went to buy cigarettes. She won't be gone long."

"I have to leave. I'll be in trouble if I don't get going," I said with a quick goodbye and started walking toward the highway. My house was less than half a mile away.

"If you don't come back, I'll sic my dogs on you!"

I kept walking. She opened the front gate and yelled, "Get her, get her!" I didn't look back until the barking got close. Moments later, I was knocked to the ground, and was being nipped all over. One dog caught his tooth in my shirt and it began to tear. With the dust churning I curled into a ball, covering my face and head with my arms. I felt the grittiness of the sand in my eyes. Suddenly, I heard a loud yelp from one of the dogs. I looked up and saw the silhouette of a man standing there holding a tire iron. The sun was setting just behind him and I couldn't make out his face. He struck again. Another yelp and the dog ran off followed by the others. Dina screamed from the front yard, "Don't you hurt my dogs!"

This kind man helped me up and gently brushed the dirt off my clothes. There were spots of blood surfacing on my shirt, mixing in with the plaid.

"You looked like you needed some help. Do you need a lift home?"

"No, I'm okay. Thanks," I mumbled. After he put his tire iron back in his trunk, he drove away in a green Pontiac. I never saw him again. I sobbed on the way home, not from the bites, but from feeling betrayed by someone I thought was my friend. My eyes were red and my nose was still running when I walked into the house. Dad was working that night. Mom glanced at me and then did a double take. I knew she'd be upset about my clothes. Everyone was already around the dinner table. I motioned to Mom to come and talk to me in private. I didn't want to talk about it at the table and scare the younger ones. Then I hurried up the stairs, peeled off my clothes and surveyed the damage. None of the bites looked bad enough for stitches. The alcohol stung just the same as I dabbed it on, wincing. I had learned from observation in seeing my younger siblings get hurt just what was a "you're okay" versus a "we're going to the hospital" injury. Later, I heard Mom on the phone asking, "Have your dogs had their shots? That's good. Oh, and Beth will not be coming over anymore." That was Mom, cool and collected. I had no idea then that in the future, encountering a German Shepherd or a Doberman would cause panic attacks.

Chapter 4

INDOOR ICE RINK: A SKATER'S PARADISE

I belonged to a Brownie troop, and later was a Girl Scout. A very nice girl named Sheri lived across the lake from me. In fact, we had gone through the early elementary school years together and her mother was our troop leader for a time. Sheri grew up in a busy household too; she had four siblings herself. Her mom donated her time to teach us interesting things that would benefit us later in life. Setting a proper table was one of several projects, as was making candles. Sheri and I enjoyed our time together and we would play together and spend nights at each other's homes. One evening, her mother asked, "How would you like to ride to the ice rink? I need to pick up Sheri's older sister from her skating lesson." I had never seen an indoor rink before. My ice rink was the lake. When we arrived, Sheri and I took our places at the rink's edge. I soaked up the sights and sounds of the entire experience with a thirst. We intently watched while a skating coach remained out on the ice with Sheri's sister, Marilyn. Both of them seemed oblivious of observers. I marveled at Marilyn's gracefulness and speed. She skated over to us showering our coats with ice shavings caused by a purposeful, quick stop. That visit changed me. I now knew what I wanted to do – take skating lessons.

Yes, I could fool around on skates in the winter on our blessed lake. I even jumped barrels. I filled in as goalie when the boys wanted to play hockey. But, I couldn't replicate that grace. I needed lessons. That night, when I was dropped off at home, I barely contained my excitement. "Mom, I saw the most wonderful thing tonight. I got to see where Sheri's sister takes her ice skating lessons. It's indoors! No snow to shovel, either. Can I take lessons, Mom? I promise I'll practice a lot."

"Beth, we're already paying for your piano lessons, honey. You have brothers and sisters to think of, too. I'm sorry, but no skating lessons."

"But, I don't like my piano lessons. My teacher has bad breath, and that mustache. She wears her nails long and they always click on the keys. And I'm not learning that much."

"Honey, you just need to practice like your sister."

It was a losing battle. I went to bed that night, but couldn't fall asleep. All I could think of was how I would feel out on the ice turning circles in a short skating skirt. Would I look graceful, too? I couldn't walk through a door without smacking my hip bone on the doorknob. I think they call that being a "klutz." Yes, a left-handed klutz at that. I needed a plan.

Chapter 5

IN SEARCH OF DICK BUTTON

I was determined to find a way to become a good skater, maybe even good enough to try out for one of the ice shows. I decided that if anyone could teach me to skate, Dick Button could. He was well-known even then as a champion skater. He still has a presence at the Winter Olympics. I asked Mom for a ride to the library on Saturday. At first, she looked shocked, but then her face broke into a smile. She really had no clue what I was after. Was I turning studious? Yes, in a manner of sorts. It turned into a field trip with younger sisters tagging along.

It took awhile, but I emerged victorious. I was clutching Dick Button's book to my chest as I confidently strode to the check-out desk. The librarian perused the cover.

"Hmmm . . . this reading might be a little technical for you, dear."

"I'll figure it out," I said confidently.

That evening, in the bedroom I shared with two of my sisters, Robin and Leesa, I sat staring at an old typewriter pondering how to tackle my personal assignment. Soon I was transferring the intricacies of several styles of strokes and stops on ice from Dick's book onto three by five cards. Cards containing various jumps and spins would have to wait until I conquered the Klutz Factor.

Other books on skating followed, but I used those three by five cards each winter until I was eighteen. They traveled with me in my coat pocket each time there was decent ice on the lake. I would read each card over and over to refresh my memory, quietly concentrating first and foremost, on grace.

Chapter 6

CHEERLEADING WAS NOTHING TO CHEER ABOUT

One of life's big decisions for girls in junior high and high school is whether to try out for the cheerleading squad. I was no different. Cheerleaders appeared to have lots of fun together. They were able to attend all of the games. It seemed to set the tone in junior high. I wanted to be accepted. I was strong and athletic. I could do this. My friend Sheri was trying out, too.

Tryouts were nerve-wracking. With the number ten pinned to my chest, I went through all the jumps and gyrations necessary and ended up being chosen as the team's alternate. I still attended all the practices and kept my uniform ready and waiting in case a girl called in sick, which did happen on occasion. The practices were held at a different cheerleader's home each week throughout the season. When it was my turn, Mom made a point of buying fresh apple cider and cinnamon donuts for us. Afterwards, there were times that a parent would need to drive some of the girls home.

My dad had bought Mom a GMC Suburban which was good-sized and felt like a minibus inside. It was dark blue-green metallic and we loved it. It was perfect for our big family. But, there were nasty comments from some of the girls on the squad. This dark undertone seemed to be lurking. First it was, "Cider and donuts?" Is that the best she could do?" Then comments regarding our car were, "How come her mom has to drive that stupid truck? Are we going to have to ride home in that? It's embarrassing. It's just ugly."

It was hurtful, seeming really petty and small. So, I guess I shouldn't have been surprised the day I was called into the cheerleading coach's office following a group practice at the school.

"Beth, some of the girls on the squad feel that you just don't fit in. They are requesting that you be replaced. Since I want to keep our squad together and happy, I'm asking that you turn in your uniform tomorrow. I'm sorry."

I was stunned. I attempted to swallow, but the lump in my throat wouldn't let me. My mouth felt like cotton. "Did I do something wrong? If I did, please tell me."

"No, I think it's just the mix of personalities, that's all. Don't take it too hard. Girls will be girls." I thought it was cold and callous. But, the clique had spoken.

The tears in my eyes stung as I walked out of her office and past the squad. A couple of giggles and snickering were the last things I remember hearing as I passed by. No one ever spoke of it again, not even my friend, Sheri. She was a cheerleader, too. We were never close again.

Chapter 7

DROWNING IN FLANNEL

In the summer of 1965, any sunny day was a great day to enjoy being outdoors, especially on the water. A new neighbor had moved in next door with her older brother and her parents. Her name was Sherry Shelton. Sherry was a year ahead of me in high school. She was a tall, thin, lively person with an infectious smile, and a love of dancing and water skiing. Her folks had decided to move out of Pontiac and into the suburbs, actually nicknamed "the sticks" by friends who were city dwellers. It was away from some of the inner city problems, especially within the high schools. Waterford schools seemed much more docile.

Sherry and I loaded up our swimming gear and headed over to Larry's house, the home of my sister Terry's boyfriend. He lived on Sylvan Lake with his father, brother and maternal grandparents. Since it was a summer weekday, the lake had very few boaters out. Terry had arrived earlier with Larry.

The boat, nestled in the placid water was a beautiful wood inboard with its finish gleaming in the sun. As Sherry and I started down the sloping, well-manicured lawn to the water, a surprise was waiting. There on the grass was a gigantic inner tube which we would find out later, came from the tire of a large road grader. Where Larry got it he didn't say.

"I can give you a ride on that you'll never forget!" Larry boasted.

Feeling fearless as we quizzically examined our newest water conquest, Sherry and I soon found out the complications of riding this monstrosity. The center of the tube was huge; it would take both of us sitting in it pushing with straight legs to be able to maintain position.

"You'll both have to hang on for dear life. Oh, and here, put on these shirts. The rubber is so coarse that when you bounce, it'll rub your skin right off," Larry declared. Personally, I was impressed that a guy would give any consideration to a female's skin. The shirts were plaid flannel, and very big.

Soon, the tube was tied onto the end of a ski tow rope with the other end of the rope looped off the boat's stern. Sherry and I were giddy with laughter, both from excitement and fear as the boat slowly began its ominous journey heading out toward the deeper area of the lake. We each had a "bronco rope" to hold onto for stability and wore thin lifebelts on our waists.

Suddenly, the growl of the husky boat engine intensified and with a roar we became nearly airborne, wedged in the tube opening, only settling on the wave tops for split seconds, and becoming airborne once again. We were hanging on for dear life. It was so frightening and we were moving so fast. Soon Sherry was laughing uncontrollably. She lost her grip on her rope and flew out of the tube and into the waves behind me. Frantically, I turned and looked back, only to see Sherry appearing smaller and smaller in the distance while waving her arms, waiting to be picked up. But the boat barreled on. Where was the spotter in the boat? Ahead was the group of waves destined to be my solo collision course.

When the tube hit the first two waves in succession, I was thrown into the air, out of the security of the tube's immense center. The bronco rope let me pull myself back toward the tube, but this time I went through the tube center, plunging into the water legs first, then the trunk, and last, my head. My path was to be different than Sherry's. Just wait for the boat to stop, I told myself. But the boat wasn't stopping. Suddenly, I was jerked into forward motion, at lightning speed behind the boat, this time totally immersed under water. The flannel shirt that was to "save" my skin, was now caught over the hook shaped inner tube valve. I was being dragged under water, caught underneath the tube. The life belt was no good to me now.

The pressure of the water was forcing my eyes open. The blurred turquoise green color surrounding me now seemed surreal. But I hadn't gotten a good breath of air while above the surface and panic was setting in. My arms felt as if they were invisibly pinned back. I could not move them let alone raise them. I desperately needed to help myself, but the water continued to push with such force as it gushed passed me. My neck was now feeling the strain. My head lowered, and now my eyelids were pushed tightly shut. I had held my breath as long as I possibly could.

At first I thought it was hallucinations, but I quickly realized the "your life flashes before your eyes" business was now becoming my reality. I was seeing birthdays, family get-togethers, Christmases with Mom, Dad, and all of the kids, Easter baskets, even visits to cousins. It was an eerie scene of 8mm film on fast-forward, whizzing through my brain at breakneck speed. The film sequence suddenly went dim. I heard my heartbeat pounding loudly in each ear, and felt as if my eardrums would explode. The last memory I had was seeing a dark, foreboding purple hue of color under my eyelids before releasing the last bit of air from my lungs.

In the meantime, Terry and Larry began scanning their path and spotted Sherry far back. Larry had swung the boat around without slowing down and headed back to get her, unaware I was being dragged under the tube the entire way. When the boat pulled aside Sherry, Larry asked, "Where's Beth?"

"She was still on the tube when I got bucked off," Sherry replied.

"Well, – we didn't see her on the way back here."

"Get in, Sherry, and we'll go look for her," Larry declared. As he began to pull in the tow rope to get the tube onto the boat, there seemed to be a resistant tugging. That's when he spotted the flannel plaid hooked over the inner tube valve.

The shirt was pulled part way off my shoulders, the buttons all still intact. The lifebelt was now encircling my chest and was also caught on the valve. I was hoisted up the back of the boat with water drooling out of my mouth. Larry lost his grip and I was dropped onto the stern of the boat, striking my lower chest and stomach. I began to choke and vomit and gasp for air all at once, cough, catch a breath and throw up and cough up more and more water. No one said anything.

I sat huddled in the back seat clutching myself in between gagging, trying not to throw up in the boat. My lips were purple, my fingers numb. We rode slowly back to shore in silence. I was convinced that my first near-death experience was just that – "near death." There's a picture in my photo album taken shortly afterward with sunken eyeballs, me curled up in the center of my deathtrap, still wearing plaid.

Chapter 8

SEWING MANIA

In junior high, I attended our ninth grade banquet, the first truly dressy event I'd been to except for an occasional wedding. We were allowed to bring a guest and I asked a nice-looking blond named Craig to go with me. I had met him on the lake with a few of his friends and was instantly attracted to him, especially his low, smoky voice. It was incredibly sexy. After pouring over pages and pages of dresses in the catalogs, I settled on a flowing pale yellow knee-length dress with long see-through sleeves from J.C. Penny's. After arriving with my beau for the evening and much to my dismay, I spotted Peggy, a classmate, wearing the identical dress. I mumbled something to her about having "great taste" and swore it would never happen to me again. And it didn't.

It's because my friend, Karen taught me how to sew. Karen was a great gal, fun loving, and talented. Between her mother and herself, they got me through the complexities of pattern reading and interpretation, preshrinking material, straightening grains, and sewing machine threading frustrations. We actually had fun whipping up dresses and skirts for school. With money for school clothes being limited it became a godsend. Mom had a sewing machine in a large cabinet in the back bedroom. I wanted to be able to sew up in my room, so when I was fifteen, I was able to purchase my first sewing machine, a Singer, on a payment plan funded from babysitting and part-time jobs. All of my homecoming and prom dresses became designed and custom made. No more concern about running into my "double" at a special function. There's nothing more satisfying than getting a compliment on a garment and being able to say, "I made it special for tonight," or "I put this together for three bucks!" Sewing would end up being an integral part of my life, a relaxing and satisfying hobby that I have always been able to put to good use. I will always be grateful to Karen for her diligence and patience. She was a gem.

Chapter 9

BREASTS AND BAREFOOT ON THE GOLF COURSE

I grew up less than a mile from Pontiac Country Club in Waterford. I don't recall what spurred me to try the game of golf. All I know is that my friend Pam and I went one day, rented clubs, bought three golf balls each and tried our hand at it. We played a few times, me left-handed, her right-handed, me less than buxom, her hugely buxom and attracting attention. We were fairly good for having no lessons. The third time out, I proceeded to hit all three of my golf balls over the left fence, a block down into the neighborhood. Frustrated, I returned my left-handed clubs to the clubhouse, grabbed some right-handed clubs, bought three more balls, and swore I would never play left-handed again. I never have. But, I was hooked on golf. I bought myself a set of starter clubs and never looked back. We played together for a couple of summers, always shedding our shoes and playing barefoot once we were out of view of the starter. Pam walked and talked like Marilyn Monroe. She was blonde, too. Men would stand at the window inside the clubhouse "gawking" while she hit a great tee shot in spite of her immense bust size. But then, it was MY turn. She was a hard act to follow and I still get intimidated teeing off near any clubhouse.

One, day, we met up with a couple of "older" guys, Frank and Andy. Frank was a teacher at a catholic school, and lived only a half mile from me although we'd never met. Andy was a good buddy of his. Pam and Andy seemed to be hitting it off, so we were "paired" but would still make small bets on the course, girls against the guys. The second time we all played together, Frank came up with a wager.

"Hey, how about we play for something more than quarters? Tell you what, let's play for our virginity. We win and you lose your virginity, O.K.? You win and we lose ours, deal?"

Somehow, I didn't picture these two still being virgins. I was a virgin. I couldn't speak for my friend. Pam chattered, "Sure, we'll do it – give us five strokes each – no problem," as she nervously giggled, sounding like a chipmunk.

I didn't want to sound wimpish, but the payout seemed steep and I took betting on the golf course seriously. I spoke up and said, "When Pam and I WIN, we will have the OPTION of taking your virginity, right?" Some grumbling ensued, but we played the match, winning by a stroke on the final hole with me sweating bullets. We kissed the boys goodbye and that's all. Frank was a great kisser and his mouth tasted pleasantly like vanilla which confounded me. Was he gargling vanilla extract in the men's room? I came as a virgin and I left a virgin, and recalling a saying that it's never wise to bet more than you can afford to lose – so much for high stakes betting.

Chapter 10

A FALL THROUGH THE ICE AND FROM GRACE

In the winter of 1966, the lake had gone through several unusual freezes and thaws. When it snowed, we would shovel off a big ice rink. Then an overnight thaw would leave just an ice ridge surrounding the rink, and the rink itself covered in water. A day or so later, the ice would refreeze, and once again, we would return to ice skating. Everyone in the family really enjoyed it except Mom. I honestly don't even know if she had ice skates. She was always concerned about us, her children having what we needed. She was so giving.

On this particular sunny day, there were a bunch of us playing a type of tag on skates, and we were equally divided into two teams. Mom cautiously walked out onto the slick ice with my brother, John. He was about three and a half and the youngest, the baby of the family. He had always been a happy, constant wonder bringing lots of joy to the family. Mom adored him, and we were really fond of him, too. He was wearing a red snowsuit that came to a point on his head, mittens, and a tiny pair of black boots. Mom called out, "Keep an eye on your brother," and trudged carefully back to the house. John <u>would</u> fuss if he was left alone too long to entertain himself. He liked hanging out with us. As John toddled about fascinated with the slipperiness under his boots, we resumed our game.

Suddenly, there was a distraction. I heard the first sound of ice cracking maybe twenty feet away. I turned and looked in horror. I saw John going feet first through the ice, bobbing up once, and down again. Then he began to go under. I frantically skated as fast as I could toward the large unmarked rectangle ice fishing hole, but tripped six feet away, sliding up to it on my belly. Quickly pulling my mittens off, I plunged one hand into the frigid black hole. John was face up under the clear ice. Reaching for him, my baby finger snagged and caught in the peak of his hood. Thank God Mom had tied it tightly under his chin. The current was pulling him toward the nearby canal that connected Elizabeth and Crescent Lake. I couldn't believe this was happening. I was firmly tugging him back ever so carefully, praying my finger didn't slip. As he emerged, I grabbed him up into my arms and skated toward shore. He was screaming from the frigid water. There was a small embankment to climb, then the highway to cross to the house. My skate blades made a painfully gritty noise on the blacktop. John became very quiet. His lips were blue and his chin quivered in the dripping snowsuit. I climbed the porch steps briskly holding him close to me.

I began banging on the front door with my elbow. I heard the vacuum running inside. Many times Mom would lock the doors while she was cleaning. I think she needed those few minutes of solace to enjoy her clean house all alone before the herd of us returned. The noise stopped and the door swung open. She looked irritated at first, but then realized John was in my arms, soaking wet. I began babbling about the unmarked fishing hole and how he wandered over to it. She didn't want to listen just then. She grabbed him from me and tersely said, "If he had drowned, I never would have forgiven you." Then the door abruptly closed. I thought it best to stay outside. With my heart pounding and legs wobbling under me, I collapsed on the steps in despair. Tears tracked straight down my face and dripped onto the cement porch. Afterward, I would have trouble sleeping, the recurrent nightmare playing in my head causing me alarm. In those dreams, I never could save him. The most torturous part of it was him staring up at me through the ice, eyes unblinking as he drifted slowly away. I followed his path, screaming, "I'm sorry, I'm so sorry." It was gut wrenching and I would wake up covered in sweat. It went on for months.

Chapter 11

WATERFORD JUNIOR MISS SHE WAS NOT

In December of 1967, there was an opportunity to compete in the local Junior Miss Pageant and I figured, why not? A very supportive friend, Londa and I hashed it over. She was the most kind and genuine person. Yet, the best part of our relationship was that we could compete with each other as friends in a noncompetitive, "Go for it!" way. We met in junior high, and along with a fun gal named Patty, the three of us did comedy skits pantomiming to entertainer Jonathon Winters. Patty was hilarious and we all shared magical moments of laughter during our home rehearsals, and later performed at the school variety shows. Londa was fairly shy when we met, but when I got involved in new things, I urged her to try experiencing them, too.

Choir was our neutral ground. We loved singing together in the school choirs and both read music and played piano. When I became involved in forensics competitions, I entered the humorous reading division. It was great fun for me trying to be both funny and entertaining. I was afforded the opportunity to continue up the ladder and compete on the state level. Londa joined in and competed, too. In turn, she took me to activities at her church where she was very involved as was her family. I never felt completely connected at the church I attended growing up. Londa and I went together to church services and retreats up north and she always made me feel welcome when meeting her friends. How refreshing.

So, we both entered the Junior Miss competition, practicing and critiquing each other. We modeled our evening dresses, trying to appear smooth and sophisticated, even when my Klutz Factor was shining faintly through. My talent competition was to be three minutes long and I had decided on a song called, "Kids" a parody on how kids make adults crazy with their antics. I had a costume in mind, envisioning a stout woman in a work dress mopping school room floors, with a scarf tying up her hair. I talked to Mom about my "costume" and she came back with one of her own dresses, quite well-worn. It would work with some stuffing, but I felt guilty wearing it, knowing possibly the day after I did, she would launder it and put it on for the day. I realized then that there were no great frills for her at the moment.

In the afternoon, all of the interviews were held. Londa and I felt pretty confident we did well. There were nine girls returning later that night for the evening gown modeling and talent competition and we were included. That evening, Mom and I rode over to the school where it was being held. As we pulled into the parking lot, Mom parked the car and then said, "Gee, I sure hope Sheri wins . . . she's such a nice girl." With that, Mom was out of the car. I was hurt and confused, stunned. Did that mean I wasn't nice enough? Not deserving enough? I didn't want to take one step out of the car. I just sat there trying to comprehend why. She opened the car door back up and said, "What are you doing? Let's go or you'll be late." I tried to put on a happy face walking through the door carrying my evening gown. Now it was torture.

I wondered what made her feel that I didn't measure up. Her opinion meant a lot to me. I never asked her to explain even though it was important to me to know.

Mom got her wish. It came down to my old friend, Sheri and me. There was a rather long delay, then we were told there was a tie and the vice principal was asked to go to the high school and check our grade point averages. Sheri's was higher and she became the new Waterford Junior Miss and wore the crown. I was runner-up and Londa came in third. We received a bracelet and a savings bond. I've kept the bracelet all these years as a reminder of that night; the competition, the comedy antics on stage that I enjoyed, and the sting of Mom's words that night.

Chapter 12

A FIRST LOVE LEAVES FOR WAR

My first true love was Al. We met at a movie night held on the Elizabeth Lake Estates Subdivision Beach across the lake from me. He was with a goofy, comedic guy named Bill and together they made me laugh. Both of them were wearing Army fatigue jackets and jeans. Al was average height, dark brown hair, big brown eyes and quite shy. On our first date, I met his folks and proceeded out to his back yard. There was a dog kennel with hunting dogs pacing in the run. On the kennel roof were two lawn chairs straddling the peak. We were going up there? It was near sunset, a puzzling site, but I went along with it. Maybe he was a romantic and we'd watch the sunset together. I was so wrong.

"I threw some bait out there in the field, some corn. It'll take a few minutes, but they'll come out" he said proudly.

"What will come out?"

"The rats will. They're big and fat. They steal the dog food we put out for our hunting dogs, but we'll get them tonight. It'll be fun."

I never thought I would be spending any evening perched on top of a doghouse shooting fat, ugly rats for sport. Then I saw the BB guns. For a first date, it was a really strange one. In the coming months, I would learn to shoot skeet and use a shotgun that would knock me to the ground and leave me with a bruised and sore shoulder for days. Al's family had a hunting cabin up north and I was allowed to go with them one weekend, my first official hunting outing with a gun. Al and his brother Tom, Al's father and I went together into the woods while Al's mother stayed at the cabin. It was a day for partridge hunting I was told. I had only seen pictures of a partridge. Curly, Al's dad was a robust man, looking part American Indian. With a full, deep voice he said I could take the first shot. As we walked ahead, suddenly the weeds began to sway and a partridge quickly fluttered into the sky. I took my shot. The bird dropped and landed on a path in front of us. But, it wasn't dead. I had hit its wing and it was badly damaged.

"Here, Beth . . . hold it like this and collapse its air sacs. It'll be quick," Curly announced.

I held the quivering bird in my hands and squeezed. The bird craned its neck a few times and I gently but quickly handed the bird back to Al's dad. Visibly irritated, Curly took the bird from me, squeezed until it was lifeless and threw it into a duffel bag. I was nauseous thinking about what I had done. I put down the gun, realizing then that my hunting days were over. There was no joy here. After taking some merciless teasing, I cleaned the dead birds alone.

Al and I attended the same high school, Waterford Township, and it was his senior school year. In the spring of 1966, I was asked to go to his Senior Prom. I had made a blue brocade three-tier dress from a Vogue pattern which became my first Vogue garment. It was classy.

When Al and I first started dating, he was working at a local gas station. My father answered the door one night when he had stopped by. Al smelled like gasoline. Dad wasn't pleased. I heard him say, "Go home and take a shower before you come around again" and closed the door. Later Al would work part-time doing drafting for the city of Pontiac. But the war in Viet Nam was in full swing. There was a draft in effect, and Al decided to enlist in the Air Force instead of waiting and wondering when he would be called. It was a tough goodbye. We had spent so much time together. By November of 1966, he was on an Air Force base. In February of 1967, he sent me a photo taken outside his barracks where three pay phones were in single file amidst drifting snow and icicles hanging from the bare tree branches. The note on the back said, "That is where I stand every time I talk to you but I guess you're worth the sacrifice!" I had heard his teeth chattering during some of our lengthy conversations as he fed quarter after quarter into the pay phone. I concentrated on school, ice skating, water skiing and sewing up a storm. Being part of a large family, there wasn't much money allocated for school clothes unless you had grown out of your size, and money from a part-time bakery job and babysitting didn't go very far. I flat out needed more of a wardrobe. I made everything but my underwear and saved a passel of money. Al and I wrote to each other two or three times a week.

He was so appreciative to receive my letters, as I was his. I really, really missed him.

By my senior year in the spring of 1968, I had no idea what I would do about Senior Prom. I had gone out briefly with Jimmy, a guy I had met in ninth grade that was transferred to a different school system for grades tenth through twelfth. He attended a different high school, the "rival" school to mine. I had always liked him and would run into him occasionally. We truly were good company for one another and if there hadn't been someone else, it could have gotten serious. He called his mother "Sarg" and enrolled in chef's class, similar to home economics for guys, and even baked my family a cherry pie. He knew my situation with Al and respected it, but did ask me if I would go to his Senior Prom. Jimmy was a happy, stocky guy and my parents really liked him, partly because we were the same age. I had been dating guys older than I was from the time I had begun to date.

While my father was keeping a lookout for a used car for me, he spotted some in Birmingham, an upscale city he drove through daily on his way home from work. The cars belonged to the Birmingham Water Department. They were all the same, 1965 Plymouth Belvederes, solid blue, a three speed on the column, vinyl seats, no radio, all having less than 30,000 miles on them. Dad told me about the cars and said I could buy one for $800.00 and he would co-sign. I was thrilled. When the paperwork was completed with my Dad, Jimmy gave me a ride to Birmingham to pick up my new used car. He drove a gold souped up and jacked up Dodge, an automatic. As we pulled into the auto lot, I popped the question.

"Hey, Jimmy, how would you like to drive my new car home? I can follow you in your car."

"You mean, this is your very first car and you don't want to drive it yourself?"

"Well . . . the truth is, I don't know how to drive a stick."

"You've got to be kidding – you bought a car that you don't know how to drive?"

"Yeah, pretty dense, eh? Well, what can I say? Can you teach me? "

"O.K., but not until we drive back to my neighborhood. I'll teach you there."

I was truly relieved. And Jim did teach me to drive a stick in his neighborhood. My father wouldn't have had the time as much as he worked. Besides, I thought Dad would have a pretty low tolerance to me grinding gears and stalling out the car. I've owned many stick shifts since, and I'm always reminded of my first experience with a clutch. That night, I got a call from Al's mother. She was one of the most entertaining women I've known. She had a sassy accent straight from the Bronx and I adored her. After Al graduated from high school, his parents moved to Bay City, which was north about 75 miles away. While Al was away in the Air Force, Al's mother, Anne and his father invited me to visit regularly. Curly called me "Wop" and why I never really knew. He just couldn't figure out my nationality, I guess. I had begun to feel like I was the daughter they never had, we were that close. She told me that Al was trying to get home for my Senior Prom so he could take me. I told Jimmy and he seemed very disappointed, but it left me nervous. Al had been gone quite awhile. Would we be the same together? I had sparsely dated, mostly double dating here and there, generally for sporting events. I hadn't even passionately kissed anyone since he left. I intended to stay a virgin saving myself for marriage, hopefully to him. I didn't take intimacy lightly and Al had honored that. He was gentle and sweet that way.

Al and I were able to attend my Senior Prom. However, on the way there, a car sped up and stayed next to us on the highway. It was Jimmy in his gold Dodge, smoking a cigar and glancing over. He had three of his buddies in the car with him. It was a pretty uncomfortable moment that turned into minutes. Suddenly he gunned his engine and sped off. Of course, Al wondered what it was all about and I told him. We didn't hide things from one another.

Al was around for just a few days, then left to return to his base hoping he would remain stateside, but overseas orders were looming and he received them upon his return. I was relieved when his assignment was in Thailand and not Viet Nam. There were too many soldiers coming home in boxes. Before he left, I had given him an eight by ten colored photo, my graduation picture which was displayed in his parents' living room and a wallet size print to carry with him. I know his folks wondered if we would get engaged before he left. We had discussed it and some of my school mates were doing just that, but we weren't really ready. I was only seventeen and I wanted it to feel right, not some rush decision, so we decided to wait. I couldn't even bear going to the airport to see him off. We said our goodbyes at his parents' house and they drove him to the airport. My high school graduation was here.

Chapter 13

THE COBO AUDITION

In the summer of 1968, I attained a position as an instructor at Holiday Health Spa (which would later be purchased by Vic Tanny.) The owner was Sonny, a petite man from the South with long dark side burns like Elvis Presley. Sonny had a vision of his female staff strutting around in French cut leotards and black spike heeled patent leather shoes. And so it became our "uniform." I was thrilled to have a summer job, but it did seem demeaning. Women were allowed at the club on Mondays, Wednesdays and Fridays, while men came on Tuesdays, Thursdays and Saturdays. I received brief training on each of the gym equipment pieces and then was responsible for teaching our clients. Right next door to us was Richardson's Farm Dairy, a small store with terrific ice cream cones. Many times, I'd work for a couple hours with women only to see them leave, walk into Richardson's momentarily and reappear with a double scoop ice cream cone in hand, licking it voraciously as they walked to their cars. If nothing else, exercising gave me the opportunity to maintain good muscle tone, especially in my legs. Water skiing and ice skating were pretty seasonal. When I and other instructors were lacking clients, we'd spend time having contests on the equipment. These girls were tough. In the months to come, I was able to horizontally press three hundred and sixty pounds. My hours were nine in the morning until nine at night three days a week with a short break midday. The balls of my feet were killing me from being in heels all day and they caused backaches – so much for feeling glamorous in heels. But Sonny insisted we only remove our shoes if a piece of gym equipment wouldn't accommodate them. I decided then that I needed higher aspirations, and that the spa would only have me for the summer.

In the early fall, there was an article in the newspaper about the Holiday On Ice show coming to Detroit, about thirty-two miles south of where I lived. They were to be here on tour at that time, first appearing at Madison Square Gardens in New York, then heading to Detroit. I was ecstatic. My mind was reeling. I wondered if I could hire on as a show seamstress and then ease into showing them I could skate? Would they give me a chance? I decided to give it a shot. I sat down that night and composed a letter to Tom Collins, the Company Manager of Holiday on Ice, billed as the "World's Largest Producer of Ice Shows." On September 21, 1968, I received my answer.

"Dear Miss Griffin:

Today I received your letter, with reference to a position with Holiday On Ice. I am very sorry to have to inform you that we do not have any positions available for people who do not skate, if you could do this there is a possibility that we would be able to use you in one of our shows. With thanks for writing Holiday on Ice, I remain...

Respectfully, Tom Collins, Mgr."

The Show would be here in Detroit the upcoming Saturday. I needed to think this through. If on Saturday, I decided to go make an appearance I knew I needed to be mentally prepared for rejection or otherwise. I decided to drive to Detroit and arrive during the matinee performance. I put on a form fitting slender summer dress I had sewn that was a pastel floral print trimmed in lace, my long hair in a French twist, and wearing heels, yes heels. If I learned anything from Sonny it was "legs can talk when they're toned." With my letter in their gold embossed envelope featuring a female skater, I parked my 65 Plymouth Belvedere, my precious Blue Funk in a lot and headed to the Cobo Arena front entrance. Speechless, as I was stopped at the top of the entrance stairs, I stuck out my envelope. With one quick glance at it by the young male attendant, his next words startled me.

"Oh, they've been waiting for you. Here, take this walkway around to the stage entrance and the guard will direct you. Nice to meet you."

I turned back and smiled at him. He began waving his arm in exaggerated movements pointing in the direction of the back of the building.

I hadn't uttered a word. They had been waiting for me? Oh, sure. As my heart picked up at a frenetic pace and with heels clicking on the sidewalk, I reached the stage entrance. A large black man wearing a security guard uniform and sporting an oversized Afro under his hat was waiting there.

"Help ya?"

Now what do I do? Fake it I told myself. You've gotten this far.

"No inglés" I said, as I thrust the envelope out, covering my address with a thumb.

"Oh man, another one that don't speak English. Well, COME-WITH-ME," talking as if I were deaf. Before, I knew it, we were standing in a big beautiful office, an inner sanctum within the bowels of this massive building. He motioned me to a chair and left. I was alone. Two minutes later, the door opened. A man in a dark suit loomed over me looking quizzically at my face.

"Well, you're beautiful, but you're not her."

I felt my face flush to beet red.

"My name's Beth Griffin. I wrote a letter about a possible seamstress position, and you mentioned that if I could skate. . ."

Suddenly, the man began to roar with laughter. I wanted to crawl under the desk.

"Well, I guess you'd like an introduction. I'm Tom Collins. We've been waiting for a lovely skater from South America to arrive today or tomorrow. My friend at the door thought you were her. It's a compliment. Now, about your letter. . . I can't really talk now. How about if I take you to my box seats? You can watch the rest of the show and I'll meet you there afterward, O.K.?"

Of course, it was okay – no, it was great! The show was flashy and beautiful. I studied the skaters, their costumes, their theatrical makeup, the feather headdresses. I felt like Cinderella at the Ball. So excitingly glamorous, I was mesmerized. Then, the orchestra played the finale and finally, warm and hearty applause. I waited awkwardly in my seat until Mr. Collins returned.

"So, you're an excellent seamstress and you can skate, too?" he asked holding my letter.

"Yes, I can," I said boldly.

"Well then, tonight can be your audition. Come back near the end of the show, before ten thirty and we'll get you on that ice and see what you can do. Here's a pass for the front door."

I didn't want to stammer. "I'll be here," I said joyously.

Driving back home over thirty miles, I had plenty of time to envision and plan. I'd wear my hair up, sophisticated, and a blue French-cut leotard from my day job. Skates, yes, I needed to polish my skates. I could hardly wait to get home and tell my folks. But, what if they weren't willing to let me drive back into Detroit that late, then what? My dad could be a bear about those things. As I pulled into the driveway, I was ready to pitch my story.

Well, I'll be. When I was finished blurting out the entire day's happenings in probably less than a minute without taking a single breath, everyone was quiet. Then Dad spoke.

"I'll sharpen your skates for you. Bring them downstairs to my workbench."

Teary-eyed with gratitude (because it meant yes, you can go) I ran upstairs to my bedroom and grabbed the department store figure skates with the dull metal blades and raced back down to the basement. My father was not easily excitable, but he seemed to be enjoying this. I had always struggled with the feeling that nothing I could do would make him proud. This was my moment.

The return trip back into Detroit had me so on edge. What if my klutziness shows through? Just be graceful, no matter what I told myself, and with that I headed for the entrance door. When the performance was over and the house lights came on, I was told to get on the ice and warm up. A couple of fellows from the orchestra who'd seen me earlier in the day started cheering me on. A woman named Ann was sent down to meet me. She studied me curiously, peering at me from behind her oversized black rimmed glasses, never showing a stitch of emotion. I began skating laps on the ice to warm up. Suddenly, I wasn't alone. A very weary looking girl with her hair in a ponytail and no makeup wearing a forest green skating outfit began skating rings around me, methodically doing jumps, difficult ones. I was way out of my league. I just wanted a spot in the chorus line, and if we were vying for the same opening, I was finished. I began to skate off the ice and over to Ann.

"I'm sorry if I wasted your time. I see you've got a much better skater than I am out here."

Ann replied, "Yes, she is but don't go because of her. She's one of the stars in the show. She took her stage makeup off and came out to practice jumps she had trouble with tonight. As Ann called out different moves in choreographic terms I didn't know, I asked her to describe the move and then I would do it.

"Where did you learn to skate?" she asked as she glanced down at my ice skates.

"I taught myself out of books. My parents couldn't afford for me to take lessons with six brothers and sisters, and I really wanted to skate. We lived across the street from a lake and I would skate every time I got the chance, learning off my homemade three by five cards."

"Wait here . . . I'll be back in a few minutes" she said rather sternly.

When Ann returned I tried to read her face to no avail. "Tell you what – you have nice lines and grace. Take some lessons from a good skating pro and let Mr. Collins know how you're doing in three to four months. We'd like to see you start next July for rehearsals in Knoxville."

I was on cloud nine.

Chapter 14

DEAR JANE, SWEET JANE

Once high school graduation was behind me and the Senior Prom was just a recent memory, the fall winds began to tug on the autumn leaves. Coolness filled the night air. Since Al had been sent overseas, there were no weekly phone calls and I missed the comfort of hearing his voice. Letters became our only form of communication. I tried buying colorful stationary to make receiving mail seem like a small celebration, and I'd spritz the letters with familiar cologne hoping to conjure up a memory or two. But, mail became frustrating with a lag time that caused our questions and answers to become disjointed. The responses were crisscrossing in the mail. It was one of those times that created an incredibly dark cloud over our relationship, a misunderstanding over words, double meanings taken the wrong way.

My Dear Jane letter arrived in December of 1968, just before Christmas. The written discussion preceding it revolved around the wanting to be intimate and the waiting seeming so long. Great, fine, I know what it's like, I wrote back. It was misconstrued as meaning I had experienced it with someone else so I already knew what it was like. Nothing could have been further from the truth. I hadn't been intimate with anyone. Once he had received my letter, he fired one back without hesitation, boasting of his exploits with multiple prostitutes in Bangkok, leaving me with a feeling that I no longer mattered to him. Then he said goodbye.

Al's mother had invited me up to Bay City to exchange Christmas presents and so she could give me my gift from Al that he had sent from overseas. It had all been arranged before I received his letter. I decided it would be better to talk to his mother in person because we had become so close. I could tell from our phone conversation that that she knew nothing about the letter.

That Saturday morning, there had been some freezing rain, then snow. My mother had asked that on my way out of town I drop my brother, Tom off at a local bowling alley to meet his Boy Scout buddies. As I turned into the parking lot, my car began to slide uncontrollably, crashing into a brick flower box. This was my first damage to my first car and I had smashed in the right front fender. Maybe if I hadn't been distracted trying to write a script in my mind of what I was going to say when I got to Al's house, maybe then I would have driven more cautiously. But the damage was already done so there was no turning back now. I felt this urgency to drive to their house and get it over with. When I reached the expressway about ten miles away, the snowstorm had worsened. Now, cars were driving half on and half off the road with the right front and rear tires attempting to grip some gravel and dirt. The seventy-nine mile ride turned into three and a half hours of stress. But, I still couldn't take a sigh of relief as I reached their driveway. There was a strange car there, unexpected company.

Al's older half brother Bob, his wife, and two daughters had decided to pop in and then saw the weather report. Driving was just too risky. We all would be spending the night. They left Sunday afternoon about three p.m. and I had grown more and more uncomfortable trying to act pleasant and happy. I was relieved when they were gone. Al's mother spoke first.

"So Betsy, (she liked calling me that) you've been awfully quiet since you got here yesterday. Are you ready to open your presents? This one's from Al. That one's from Curly and me," she said as she pulled the gifts out of a cupboard and laid them in front of me.

"Hey, what's with the long face? It's Christmastime!"

"Al broke up with me" I muttered as I stared at the green countertop, my eyes beginning to well up with tears.

"What? You're a liar! My Allen would never break up with you . . . he loves you! How can you say that?"

Suddenly I found myself fumbling around in my purse until I found his letter and dropped it onto the counter. I really didn't think she would believe me without some type of proof.

"Read it if you want," I said in a slight whisper.

Silence ensued. She seemed to read parts of it over and over. I needed to get up and blow my nose.

"That son of a bitch...what's wrong with him? He's not himself in this letter, Betsy. I don't understand!" As her voice trailed off, she nervously lit a cigarette, took a long drag and then expelled the smoke with a heavy sigh.

"I need to go home" I said wearily. "I'm sorry about all of this-
-I just couldn't tell you over the phone." Shoving the crumpled
letter back into my purse and picking up my suitcase, I slowly
trudged toward the door. Ann put her arm around my waist and
just held on.

"Don't have this be over for us too, Betsy. Curly and I love
you."

I loved them, too.

Chapter 15

COFFEE WITH COPS

After the hurt of Al's and my breakup began to subside, I was determined to get back out into the dating world and enjoy some casual dating even though it was only until I left for the ice show in July. My focus centered on one thing – living my dream ice skating, something I thought was exciting and challenging. A week after my Cobo audition, I bluffed my way through the Detroit Free Press newsroom to a sports reporter. I called and made it sound as though I worked inside and had misplaced Tim Wood's parents' phone number. Tim had been a gold medal winner at the Winter Olympics and made his home in Bloomfield Hills. I knew someone in the sports department would have the number. When I got his parents on the phone, his mother handed the phone over to his dad, Dr. Wood. I plowed through my explanation of the reason for my call.

"Hi, my name's Beth Griffin and I auditioned for Holiday on Ice last weekend. I was advised to join a good ice skating rink and take lessons for a few months. I knew if anyone could give me direction in the best place for me to start, it would be you folks. Any suggestions?"

"It's funny you called today. I'm connected with the Detroit Skating Club. You need two sponsors to join and I just happen to be sitting here with another one watching the football game."

"I'm so sorry I bothered you on Sunday. Is there a day when I could meet with both of you?"

"No time like the present. Could you come over now?"

"Absolutely!"

It was so kind of him to invite me over. I got the address, dressed up in my lucky dress, hair back up in a French twist and headed for the Wood house. There, I met with the two wonderful gentlemen on the Board of Detroit Skating Club who approved my joining and I was in business. Now, I just needed to find a skating pro.

After that, my days were spent working at a local bank in home improvement loans and evenings on the ice practicing for several hours. I was so fortunate to meet Ron, my teaching pro. He had red hair and freckles and he was busy training a brother and sister duo for the Olympic pairs competition. I felt honored he would bother with me. The rink was nearly an hour drive home, and twice I fell asleep at the wheel on the John Lodge Expressway from fatigue. But nearby there was an incredible bagel shop on Eight Mile, and I'd pick up the most spectacular and delicious salted bagels hot out-of-the-oven. That was dinner many nights, as the rink would close at dinnertime then reopen later. I had nowhere to go and parts of the area weren't very safe. It was a few years afterward that the ice rink fell victim to arson and burnt to the ground.

A very fun guy named Tom with a nickname of "Froggie" and I met at a local dance. I loved dancing and he was a good dancer. Shortly after, I spent some spare time with him teaching me the finer points of shooting pool. We had a lot of fun practicing on a bumper pool table in his parents' basement. Then one night I got a phone call from him.

"Hey, seems like you're ready to shoot some pool in a pool hall, so let's try it tonight, okay? Wear a plaid skirt if you have one and some knee socks. See you at seven."

Did he say a plaid skirt and knee socks? It sounded like private girls school stuff. Why would he want me to look like I just got home too late to change my clothes? Well, it didn't take long to find out.

"It makes you look pretty innocent. Nobody will guess you're a good pool player. It's so much easier to take their money," Tom chuckled.

And was he right. Guys would make some wise-cracks about it being past my bedtime or didn't I have homework to do. I'd yawn on cue, then Tom would challenge them to play us, and we'd walk away with the money. It was great fun, euphoric. Not long after, some of our dates were being funded thanks to the guys who couldn't turn down a chance to beat us. Once or twice a week, Tom played basketball at a church only a few miles from the ice rink, so he would drive to the church with me in tow and say, "Take my car and pick me up when you're finished with practice. See you later."

I'd freak. I wasn't comfortable having someone entrust me with their car. It was a beautiful blue Cadillac Eldorado – my favorite color. I was so concerned someone on Seven Mile would like it as much as I did and it would be gone when I came out of the rink. But each time it was there. It was really nice having someone else to be with riding home. Tom was really sweet and thoughtful and had such a calm demeanor. Chewing on a toothpick many nights seemed to be one of his trademarks.

One night, Tom and I walked into a local Big Boy Restaurant and as we passed one of the booths, a voice asked, "What's your hurry?"

I glanced over and it was Larry, my older sister's boyfriend sitting there in a navy blue police uniform having coffee and a snack with his partner. Tom and Larry seemed to know one another and then we met his partner, Ray. They were both on the Pontiac Police Force just like my Uncle Bill. The conversation was short. Ray was grinning and when he spoke, I liked his voice. It was low, distinct, and husky. I've always been attracted to the "radio voice" even if stature and voice didn't seem to be a match. Five years earlier, Craig, the boy I took with me to the eighth grade banquet had that same voice, so low and smooth, but rich and husky. It was such a turn on.

A day later, my sister Terry asked me what I thought of Larry's partner, Ray. Larry had been filling him in based on what he knew.

"He wants to know if you'll have coffee with him. What do you think?"

"Ah, sure, I guess." The "ouch "of Al still hadn't left me, but I was determined to enjoy myself. After all, I was going to be leaving town in the summer. Tom was really a joy to be around and he hadn't been pushy about intimacy. Nothing serious for me, not now, I told myself. I was hoping Ray would be the same and just keep it light. The next evening, Ray called and we arranged to meet for coffee and conversation.

Chapter 16

LESSONS AND PRACTICE IN LOVE, LIFE, AND WAITRESSING

In the fall after my high school graduation and before Al and my breakup, I had considered joining the Air Force. Al was there and it seemed to agree with him and I felt a sense of duty to contribute somehow. I had talked with a recruiter, as I felt I was young, athletic, and somewhat bright and would be an attribute to the military. At the time, the Viet Nam War was still in full swing and there was a draft based on what number young men were issued after their eighteenth birthday when they registered. A high number meant a relatively safe position; many felt a low number could be a death sentence. Girls had no worries about the draft. We just were there to wave goodbye as these young aspiring men left for the War. Because so many young people had decided to make a choice regarding which branch of the service to enter, the Air Force at the time was backlogged with applicants. I was told I would be receiving paperwork in the mail as soon as things were caught up. But, when the opportunity for auditioning for the ice show came, I wasn't sure what I would do if and when I heard from the Air Force.

I continued to date both Tom and Ray until one evening I boxed myself into a corner time- wise and ended up with two dates within hours of each other. I felt terrible about it and went to Tom and talked to him about the situation. Ray had certainly become more and more affectionate and I wasn't feeling right about seeing both of them. What I know now that I didn't know then was that there would have been no discussion about this with Ray. This I know. He would have become enraged. Tom was the ever-present gentleman and wished me the best telling me, "Do what you have to do." I had been skating and training now for several months. The last thing Tom did for me is have me pose in his living room and he took my picture in a skating outfit to mail back to Tom Collins at Holiday on Ice. The picture was sent along with a letter my skating pro, Ron had written verifying my training and skill level I had attained.

In March of 1969, my answer came in the mail. I was upstairs in my room after three days of retching and diarrhea from the worst stomach flu ever. No one wanted to come up and hand me the mail that had arrived. I felt quarantined. I believe a younger brother braved it and brought the mail up as he was home just getting over the same thing. When I opened the envelope with the embossed picture of a young female skater on the corner, it contained both a short letter from Mr. Collins and my skating contract. I heard my father's voice in the hallway downstairs. He had just gotten home from work that morning. I tried to call to him, but my voice was so weak I barely made a noise. I called out to him three times and that last time he heard me.

"Dad, I got a letter from the ice show, and they sent my skating contract." There was a long pause and then he said quietly, "That's good." For being so ill, it was indeed a happy day.

I knew leading up to the time of my departure coming in July, I needed to find a different position. My boss at the bank had been drinking heavily on his lunch hours and we younger women in the office were having to deal with his roaming hands and slurred speech. I also had lost interest in my work and I knew I could get more ice time with a different job.

It was spring and the golf courses were opening up. I took a waitressing position at a local golf course/restaurant whose owner was a tyrant. I had an epiphany because of the experience. Everybody should be a member of the wait staff once in his or her life. It should be a rule, maybe even a graduation requirement. We would all have more respect for the profession and would all understand the meaning behind decent tipping. Our boss had a requirement; a large service tray loaded with dirty dishes had to contain at least thirty pounds of dishes on it, or he would demand you return it to the dining area until it contained the "appropriate amount." The tray would actually be weighed if it looked a little "light." What was the reason for it? No one really knew. What we did know was that the trays had to be hoisted up by your arms onto your shoulders with thirty or more pounds on them each time which got to be tiring. Also, if there was an accident with a tray where even one dish was broken, you were charged for it. If a drunk staggered into you toppling your tray, oh well. There were weeks that waitresses owed the boss money and it was withheld from their checks. He was a disgusting pig. Each morning, a different waitress was assigned to use urn cleaner in the coffee pots and to make the coffee. If the boss didn't particularly like the coffee you made he would bellow loud enough to be heard out in the dining room. It was embarrassing. One morning a gal named Linda came rushing in late, and knowing the boss would be in at any time, threw the urn cleaner in and ran for her apron. Well, Mr. Wonderful came around the corner, drew a cup and took a healthy slug of "coffee" and began fuming and sputtering profanities when he choked on urn cleaner. We were laughing so hard, we thought we'd wet our pants. Needless to say, Linda was fired, we were all warned, and life went on.

My one perk of working there was free golf. The course was very strange, but it was a course. At least some days I could get nine holes in before heading to the ice rink. There were days when groups of soldiers from the Nike Base nearby came to play a round of golf. The Nike Base was an underground missile base and it was quite secretive back in the 1960's. There was a non-commissioned officer I nicknamed Teddy Bear. He just had that look about him and his soldiers really liked him. One day, a group of us played golf together and since he had misplaced his putter he borrowed mine. After the match was over, I had to hurry to get to the rink, but before I left, he asked me if I would go to a party with him the following evening. We didn't have time to discuss it right then and I asked him if he could call me later.

I was torn. Ray wanted to spend more time with me as my departure date was just weeks away. Ray and I had become intimate even though I had wanted things to remain light-hearted. After all, I was leaving town. It was my mistake to let things get out of control and it's difficult to back up. Because of it, I felt I had to decline Teddy Bear's offer even though the thought of going out with an officer was enticing. We talked on the phone that evening and he was very disappointed. The following day, I didn't have to work but I hadn't gotten my putter back from Teddy Bear. I drove to the course and ran into two of his soldiers in the bar. There was this air of gloom.

"Where's the Teddy Bear?" I asked.

"Like you care," one of them snarled at me.

"You should have gone with him last night," another one said. "He wouldn't have gotten drunk if you had gone with him. He really wanted you to go."

"So, what are you telling me? He's got a big hangover and it's my fault?" I asked.

"No, he's in the hospital in a coma. He smashed his car into tree last night and no one found him until a paperboy went by on a bike this morning. He's in Intensive Care. His mom's flying in today. If you would've gone with him this wouldn't have ever happened."

Would I have let him drive after drinking so much? Would he have insisted on driving anyway? Would he have had that much booze if I had been with him? By not being with him, did I save my own life? His friends' comments left me saddened and with many unanswered questions.

I got the name of the hospital. It was where I had been a "candy striper" for three years doing volunteer work. I immediately drove there and went to the ICU waiting room. That's where I met his mother. She was trying not to cry as we talked. She said he was on life support but had severe injuries. He died the next day. His soldier buddies returned my putter. I knew I shouldn't feel guilty, but a part of me did just the same.

Chapter 17

HOLIDAY ON ICE AWAITS AND WAITS

As my departure date of July 6, 1969 loomed, I became increasingly both excited and yet leery of how I would be handling my goodbye with Ray. I had every intention of staying in close contact with him. Besides, the Show was to start the tour in New York City and the second stop would be in Detroit. Those three months should fly by.

I also had a terrible scare earlier in the spring. I was at the rink waiting for two hockey teams to finish their game. Finally, the Zamboni machine was released onto the ice for resurfacing. When all was finished, many of us scrambled to get our own personal markings into the freshly manicured ice. I began practicing one of my jumps and as I landed, my skate blade dropped into a crack in the ice; a crack—this was something I had never seen at Detroit Skating Club. Somehow though, I was the one who fell into it. My body was still in rotation with my left leg pointing forward and the rest of me turning backward. There was such a torturous wrenching in my left knee that I collapsed onto the ice. I was told early on that there was an unwritten rule regarding someone going down onto the ice; you are to get up without help. After all, when you're performing and it should happen, you would have to get yourself up off the ice then, too. So, I sat on the ice until my rear end began to burn from it. I was afraid I wouldn't be able to put any weight on my left leg and contemplating my predicament kept me from thinking about the pain. A young boy became concerned and skated over to ask me if he should go get my instructor. I reluctantly agreed. After all, I didn't want to seem like a wimp but frozen fanny gets uncomfortable, too. My pro came over looking concerned and I showed him the crack in the ice so he could warn other students. He said that helping me off the ice today was an exception and to head home.

This was the second time in my life I had wished my car had an automatic shift instead of a stick shift. I was only able to push in the clutch one time and my knee throbbed with pain. Since my car required double clutching from first to second gear, it compounded the problem. It was out of the question, so I drove the twenty plus miles home on the expressway in second gear. It was a long and painful ride. As I hobbled into the house and up the stairs to bed, I wondered how serious the injury was. I fell asleep purely from exhaustion with an ice pack perched on top of my knee.

The next morning, the pain woke me up with a vengeance. I threw back the covers and realized my left knee resembled a hot soccer ball. It was so stiff that I could barely walk. Suddenly, my fantastic dream of the ice show was looking seriously challenged. My mother called an orthopedic M.D., Dr. "R" who saw me that day. I explained to him all in one breath what had happened and how I needed to be back on the ice immediately, that there was a contract riding on it.

"Well, I'm going to have to use this syringe (which looked huge) to draw the fluid off your knee. This will hurt a little bit."

He filled the syringe several times and the drainage was bloody dark red. Not a good sign, he said. The cortisone came next. Immediately after the injection, my knee felt cool and almost normal. I returned to have it drained over the next several weeks and gradually the drainage lightened up in color. There had a total of three cortisone injections.

"No more cortisone, Beth. That's it. And you might as well know, if you fall and re-injure this knee, you may never be skating on it again without having surgery. I know it's important to you. So, good luck."

When I was able to return to the rink, my sense of confidence was flawed and losing my balance made me panic. I felt like my future depended on the avoidance of any act of klutziness. Who me? After several weeks, Dr. R agreed that I could return to the rink to do laps and nothing else – no jumps, no spins. I turned to ice dancing which kept me on the ice and I got the chance to get to know Ron and Cindy, the Olympic skaters better. Ron had a beautiful two-tone 1950's Chevy, turquoise and white. Ron was very tall, probably six feet four and Cindy was about five feet and weighed barely one hundred pounds if that. One night on the ice, Ron said, "Hey let me try a lift with you." I balked at it because I've always weighed more than people would think.

"Hmmm, Ron . . . I'm pretty sure I'll be harder to lift than your sister."

"Oh, come on, what's the harm? Let me see what I can do." On the next lap around the rink, he tried hoisting me above his head. I heard him groan, "Oh my <u>gosh</u>, how much do you weigh?"

"One hundred thirty-one, Ron," as he set me back on the ice. I was afraid I'd given him a hernia. We never did any lifts after that.

I did have one major disappointment regarding all of the time and effort I had made to become this skater I wanted to be. Neither of my parents ever saw one of my lessons nor had they ever been to Detroit Skating Club. After all, I was eighteen and paying my own way and I shouldn't have let it bother me. It seemed selfish. There were five younger children still at home. Dad was working so much, seven days a week at times and Mom had to be the matriarch at home so there were reasons. I did, however catch them together a few days before my planned departure to talk to them about something really important to me.

"I'd like to know if you'll promise me something that would really mean a lot. I need you to take me to the airport, no one else. I've worked so hard for this and I don't want anything screwing it up. I know Ray will want to take me and I can't have that. Will you promise me?"

"Sure, honey. We're planning on it," Mom exclaimed with an assuring gaze.

"Good. I'm glad that's settled," as I breathed a sigh of relief. I thought my worries were over.

The Fourth of July was as grand as usual with a big picnic and fireworks on the water that evening. It was always fun hearing my younger siblings "oooohs" and "ahhhhs" at the colorful sparkles in the night sky. My birthday was the day before, but I generally got my birthday cake presentation on the Fourth when we were all together. Mom still did the candle thing, even with me turning nineteen. My sister Terry's boyfriend, Larry, the policeman was there and asked me if I had heard from Al. After Al broke it off with me, I received one letter from him about two months later stating he had a change of heart and wanted me back in his life. I was angry and hurt and somewhat relieved that I would already be in Knoxville with the show by the time he returned from overseas. I never replied to his letter. I asked Larry why he brought Al up.

"Well, he's been home for three weeks. Didn't you know? I guess he must not care about seeing you."

It took me totally by surprise, yet I was peeved. I was tempted to call him up at his parents' house in Bay City and give him a piece of my mind, but I didn't do it. No emotional rollercoaster tonight. No thank you.

That evening I began to pack for my upcoming adventure. I had bought some colorful floral luggage to avoid baggage mix ups. The butterflies in my stomach had already begun. The next day was for tying up loose ends. I turned my car over to Dad, took my last swim and slalom skied around the lake, and then went out on my last date with Ray that evening. It was hard saying goodbye, yet we managed to stay upbeat for most of the evening. I gave him a box of colognes from all over the world as a parting gift. But it was a "goodbye for now" as I closed the front door. I watched him get into his navy blue Grand Prix and pull onto Cooley Lake Road with tail lights glowing as he slowly drove away.

I barely got a wink of sleep that night with all the excitement that awaited me. I hoped that I would be able to sleep on the plane. It was nearly eleven in the morning when I came down the stairs packed and ready with luggage in hand and wearing a sleeveless pale green dress and heels. I asked Dad if the whole family was going or would it be just him, Mom and me. Before he could answer I heard a car pull into the driveway. It was Ray.

"What is he doing here? I said goodbye to him last night. You and Mom promised me you would take me!" I ranted at Dad as my face began to flush. There was knocking on the front door.

"Beth, Ray said he didn't mind driving you and offered to save us the trip. He just called this morning while you were finishing packing," Dad said definitively.

"No, no – it's not supposed to be like this. I've dreamed about this day. I don't want it to be different. Would you PLEASE take me?" I pleaded.

"Hon, we already told Ray it was okay," Mom replied. My attempts were doomed. Then I began to feel guilty over being an imposition to my parents. "Always put others first," I had been taught since I was young. As I began to hug each of my siblings, then Mom, and lastly Dad, I actually thought I saw a little tear in his eye, the first ever.

I begrudgingly slid into the front seat of Ray's car. My face felt hot from my tears. We didn't talk at all the first few miles. When he turned onto Telegraph Road for the thirty plus mile journey, it started.

"How can you think of leaving like this? Don't I mean anything to you? Do you know what this will do to me? You know, I thought it over last night, and if this is what you want to do to destroy us, fine. I'll leave the Police Department, join the military and if I get killed over there, it'll be on <u>your</u> head."

Oh, he knew how to push my buttons. Three of my male classmates had been killed in Viet Nam that year and he knew how sensitive I was about the War. There was no love whatsoever in the conversation, and I refused to argue with him. It continued down this path the entire ride. I felt like a prisoner in his car and was totally spent by the time we reached the terminal.

"Please . . . Ray, drop me off at the terminal door. You don't have to stay until I leave. It's fine. Let's say goodbye here."

He wouldn't have any part of it. His determination to spoil this day, my day was menacing. It continued into the terminal. I escaped to wash my face. In the bathroom staring into the mirror, I said to myself, "See Mom, see Dad, this is why I needed you to drive me here today, not Ray." Then I threw up in the sink. Finally, my flight was called over the loud speaker. The plane was boarding. Each time, I said "I have to go" Ray would say, "Not yet – you have more time." A kindly-looking older black gentleman in an airport uniform had been within earshot of us. He looked at me sympathetically and said, "Miss, that's last call for boarding." I stood up and straightened my dress.

"Goodbye, Ray."
Taking a deep breath I headed for the boarding hallway. Ray grabbed me by my elbow and clutching it, blurted out, "Okay, will you marry me?"

It was emotional blackmail. It weakened me. I missed my plane. I don't know exactly what I said, but it was an affirmation of some type.

Then my thoughts began whirling . . . do I call my parents first and tell them I didn't leave and I was staying because I was getting engaged? Do I call New York and tell them I was reneging on my contract? Would I be sued? Would I be happy? Would I GET happy? Everything was a blur.

It was now quiet in the car on the way home. Ray wanted to go by his folks' house and tell them. I didn't know what to do. I called my parents before we left the airport. There was a long silence, and then Mom said, "Well, come on home," and hung up.

The first call from New York came the next morning. Dad had answered the phone, announced New York was on the phone to my mother, and handed her the phone to give to me. They wanted to know if I had missed my flight or had been in an accident. I told them there had been a change of plans and I wouldn't be coming. I was reminded I was under legal contract and they would wait another day for me. I quietly made another plane reservation for the following day and told Ray I couldn't throw this opportunity away. He said we needed to look at rings and he wouldn't hear of me going. After all, we were getting married. I let my second reservation slip away. Dad wasn't talking to me and didn't for what seemed like a few months. His disappointment in me was very visible. I had to buy my car back from him. I had to find a job. I had to plan a wedding. I had to justify to myself what a mess I'd made of my dream just to "always put others first," and to make Ray happy at my own expense. It was a horrible beginning to something that should have been a happy, wonderful time in my life.

Chapter 18

HURTS ABOUND AS A SOLDIER RETURNS

I had gotten engaged. Like so many other girls I had attended high school with, each had their own reasons for doing it so soon after high school graduation . Age nineteen, twenty seemed pretty normal for many, but I was mourning the loss of my dream, my career I let slip away. My sister, Terry and Larry had gotten engaged and their wedding was in its final planning stages. There was no plan for me to be in the wedding because I was to be away with the ice show. Suddenly, I wasn't going anywhere, so I was back in Terry's wedding after all. I had to get fitted for a bridesmaid's dress pretty quickly. I had no job, no car, but I was sporting a new marquise diamond on the left hand. Then I got a phone call from Al.

He said he wanted to come and see me and asked if he could come that day. Our conversation was brief. I said yes. I wondered if he was coming to apologize. I wasn't even supposed to be in town. I should have been in Knoxville.

It was a hot, summer day and I sat in a lawn chair under the hickory nut tree in the front yard letting the lake breeze cool my skin. A different kind of butterflies had settled in my gut, and I nervously waited for Al to arrive. It was less than an hour when the familiar black Oldsmobile turned into the driveway. I stayed in my chair. He climbed out all tan and lean, so handsome wearing aviator sunglasses and my favorite cologne.

He stopped directly in front of me and said staring, "God, you look so beautiful. It's been a long time, hasn't it? So, what's new?"

"This is," I said rather defensively, showing him the engagement ring on my left hand. My nerves were rattled but I was determined to stay composed.

"So, how new is that?" he asked as he settled into a lawn chair and focused on the ground.

"It's been less than a week, actually." I wanted him to feel that being home for weeks and waiting so long to see me may have been really poor timing, but neither one of us brought it up. After that, there was a long silence. Then everything seemed awkward.

Casual conversation about the family turned to him mumbling something about having to get back to Bay City. Al told me to take care of myself and left. Elapsed time: eight minutes. We didn't even shake hands. I found out years later from his folks that he drove the eighty-seven miles back home in less than 40 minutes, walked into the house, picked up my eight by ten graduation picture off the coffee table and hurled it across the living room smashing it into a million pieces without saying a word.

Chapter 19

CAREER CHANGES NEEDED

I had been so confident about my career direction. Now I was facing the challenge of starting over and trying a shot at something entirely different and most likely lackluster. The hospital where I was born and had done volunteer work was about five miles away from home. I put my application in and a week later I had an appointment for an interview.

Mr. "B" was a very tall, gray haired pleasant man who oversaw the credit department at Pontiac General Hospital. I was interviewed and hired to start working alongside at least twenty other women in a large, wide open room with no cubicles. This was my first experience with a multitude of women in one big fat melting pot. It wasn't bad. We all worked hard, laughed hard and compared stories about dealing with the public, especially because of overdue accounts we handled. We each had a section of the alphabet based on patients' last names. We played jokes on each other like shaving cream on the phone mouthpiece, and shoe polish on the earpiece. It was time to be more creative. One of my best jokes was on Nancy, the biggest jokester in the office. Someone had sent me in a check and used a blank piece of stationary to fold it in. It was from a toilet seat company. I took the blank paper and typed a congratulatory letter addressed to Nancy, telling her that she had won a customized toilet seat that would play a tune when she sat on it. I mailed it to Nancy's attention at the Hospital. She was so excited when she opened it thinking she was some big winner. We were busting up with laughter.

I would stay in the Credit Department for about a year. An opportunity came up for an EKG and EEG Technician. I transferred upstairs and worked with a small group of women technicians, one of which was uncouth, unkempt and a troublemaker. Our supervisor was friendly but very passive and would just ignore our troublemaker even when she would show up for work late no nylons, dirty shoes, hair uncombed wearing a top, a wrinkled lab coat and no uniform pants because "they're all in the dirty clothes." It was gross. I was just the opposite about my appearance having pride in being neat with uniforms pressed, shoes polished. I seemed to be constantly in her line of fire and grew to intensely dislike working there.

One of our duties was to rush to the emergency room when a cardiac emergency was announced. The doctors working there were on a type of rotation. You may be seen and treated for pneumonia by a gynecologist, for instance. Most doctors had to take their turn. One especially busy day, I was called to E.R. "stat" for a woman who was brought in looking bluish gray, "cyanotic" it was called. The attending physician, a surgeon, commanded I get an EKG (electrocardiogram) and I was in the process of getting the patient connected to the machine, when the doctor, without warning or calling "all clear" decided to turn the defibrillator up full-tilt and shock her. Well, I took the entire shock. He might as well have put the paddles on my chest. It was a tremendous jolt and I was knocked back into the wall, unconscious before I hit the floor. I remember waking up and not being able to feel my arms. There were two men staring down at me.

"Hello...do you know your name? Do you know where you are? How many fingers do you see?"

It was Dr. "K" and Dr. "O" both cardiologists who had an office together. I was eventually helped off the floor. I had a headache. My arms were still buzzing. While I was out cold, the lady on the cart with the blue tinge had received her own "shock" and was doing well. I was returned to work. Being naïve about protocol, I didn't think to ask if a report would be written about what had happened. I found out much later no incident report had ever been made. I didn't even get the rest of the day off. It did, however, give me a chance to know these two doctors better, and it wasn't too long before I was approached and asked if I would consider leaving the hospital to come to work for them in their office. I took it. I could hardly wait to get out of the fray.

Chapter 20

A WEDDING TO REMEMBER

Ray and I began planning our wedding. I was all of nineteen and Ray was twenty-five. Nearly all of our friends, both cops and Ray's college friends were married. Looking back, I don't have a clue why we decided to get married in January, mid-winter and only six months away. Neither set of parents were comfortable with conversations regarding the choice of churches. I was raised in a strict Protestant missionary church but had drifted to other ones over the years – Nazarene, Lutheran, and Episcopal as these were churches where girlfriends of mine belonged. If you attended a sleep-over on a Saturday night, going to church Sunday morning was natural. Ray was raised Catholic but was non-practicing, with his father being a Catholic and his mother was Baptist. So, it was our decision to find a church that could possibly make everyone happy and that was All Saints Episcopal Church in Pontiac. We attended a counseling session with the Reverend prior to his agreement to marry us.

Mom took me aside one day and asked me a significant question.

"Your dad and I wondered if you and Ray would consider taking some money in lieu of having a big wedding. Have you thought about having just a small ceremony? "

Terry's wedding had just taken place months earlier. I was concerned the expense would be a burden. But, we decided to have a large wedding just the same in January and said we would help with some expenses. Ray and I began having small spats over supposedly insignificant things that mostly involved where I had been, who with, and what I was doing. His temper would flare, and there were times he'd do things like kick his car door or take off his watch and throw it to the pavement.

Ray was a very talkative man, very funny at times, and he knew hundreds of jokes. Years later, I would be stunned when the television show, "N.Y.P.D. Blue" hit the airwaves and I heard David Caruso's voice for the first time. It was haunting – it was so similar to Ray's and he had the reddish hair like him, too. I met many of Ray's fraternity brothers from Western Michigan University. They were from the TKE fraternity and he seemed very proud of that. I recall a classy picture of him and his fraternity brothers standing in suits amidst some really nice cars on a golf course. That was their style. One of his frat brothers ended up joining the same police force and they rode together as partners at times. He and his wife would be part of our wedding party. Ironically, that same man some years later was found guilty of murdering his second wife in grisly fashion and received life in prison. There were get-togethers with the frat brothers and their wives or girlfriends. Since all of them met in college, all were graduates – except for me.

There were also the parties with strictly policemen and their ladies. Most policemen I met preferred to relax and party with their comrades instead of outsiders. We attended a police party one night, and as we walked in the front door, Ray quickly disappeared into the crowd. Mike, the host chuckled and said, "Well, don't feel abandoned – cops are like that. Can I get you a drink? "he asked. Before I could utter a word, Ray was back, gripping my elbow, and snapped at Mike.

"Hey, don't you worry about my lady and her drink. I'll take care of that, not you."

I was stunned. Mike, who was a very easygoing guy about six feet six inches tall looked down at Ray and said "Hey man, I was just trying to be polite." Then Mike shrugged his shoulders and walked away. This possessiveness was not an attractive trait, and I wondered what triggered Ray to be rude like that. Within five minutes, I had my drink and Ray was back in the kitchen telling jokes to the guys standing in front of the refrigerator that was stacked on top with guns. That was common at police parties for the guys to put their firearms on top of the refrigerators both out of sight and out of immediate reach.

As time went by, I asked two of the fraternity brothers' wives, Jean and Gail to be bridesmaids. My sister, Leesa, also was to stand up for me and Terry was to be Matron of Honor. Cousin, Linda, was picked as my flower girl, and I made her satin dress. Brother, John, was lined up as ring bearer. With the hall, caterer, photographer, and flowers ordered, the dresses purchased and alterations completed, everything seemed to fall into place except for one big exception—the weather.

The day we were to be married was January 17, 1970. The night before, Ray had given me a wedding gift. It was a ring in brushed silver with a wide band and a beautiful sapphire nestled in the middle.

"I designed it myself," Ray said proudly. It was beautiful and thoughtful. I have it to this day.

The following day was nearly our undoing. It began snowing during the night, and the next morning on our wedding day, it snowed and snowed until many roads were impassible. Paul, Ray's best man and fellow frat brother was overseas in Viet Nam. He had been drafted almost immediately after his college graduation, but his mother was flying in from near Chicago for the wedding. Another frat brother, Jon, would be standing up in Paul's absence. Paul's mother was having difficulty getting out of Chicago because of the immense amount of snow at the airports both there and in Detroit. It was a struggle navigating anywhere.

That afternoon, I left early for the church with my bridal dress and heels in hand. I was nervous about everything – the flowers getting to the church as well as the wedding party, the guests being able to drive in such poor conditions, the caterer getting the food to the hall, the wedding cake, all of it. I was dropped off wearing my blue jeans and stepped into fourteen to eighteen inch drifts of snow. The large parking lot outside the church was completely filled with just snow, snow, and more snow. It was eerily quiet except for the whistling of the fierce wind around the corners of the building. None of the parking lot was shoveled nor was the sidewalk. I made my way through the drifts to the entrance door. It was locked. I pounded on the door and there was no response. I trudged to a side door, and pounded again with no answer. It was a nightmare in the making. Since the cell phone generation had not begun yet, looking for a pay phone was next. I turned to retrace my steps in the snow and walk toward the main street but the wind had taken care of that. No tracks in the snow. The frostbite I had suffered from in my early teens resurfaced in both feet and my toes were becoming numb. It seemed futile.

My sister, Terry arrived with Larry driving and I climbed into their car feeling defeated. Was this really going to turn out to be one of the happiest days in my life? It took some time, but I was eventually able to reach the Reverend who in turn reached the custodian who showed up and unlocked the church. By the time the parking lot was partially dug out and the sidewalk was cleared, much of the floor in the church was tracked with melting snow. The wedding party members straggled in one by one and we went to our prospective dressing room areas and hurriedly got dressed and ready. The wedding ceremony was already running late. While assembling together in the outer hallway, someone accidently walked up the back of my wedding dress train with wet shoes leaving gray footprints in the white silk and Chantilly lace.

"Beth, maybe we'll be able to fold your train over so the footprints won't show in the pictures," the understanding photographer said quietly. The church wouldn't allow the Wedding March to be played there, so the alternative music began and minutes later it was over. The pictures were taken with the footprints "folded" over into my train so they didn't show. The photographer became my hero.

The reception was another matter. Several policemen had threatened to have Ray "arrested" at the wedding reception and hauled off to jail which was a childish prank they played on each other. This was not the first impression I wanted my friends and relatives to have of Ray and my "new" group of friends. After all, there would be plenty of food and booze to keep them busy I thought. After the dinner was served and the wedding cake was cut, the quiet rumbling about it began and spread through his police buddies. At least they had waited a while. We had attended a wedding where they took the groom away at the beginning of the reception, put him in a jail cell, and he did not reappear until the reception was nearly over. He had no dinner, no cutting of the cake, and nearly no pictures. Ray had warned them it better not happen, which was of course, more reason to follow through. Ray's temper could be volatile; it was a show we could do without. I went out into the hall corridor and began pacing. Ray's godmother, Sue and her grown son, Phil were there and had offered to drive our getaway car if and when the time came and we were ready to leave for the evening. I was so nervous I asked Phil for a cigar and began rapidly puffing on the tiparillo. Then, the yelling began. I opened the door leading into the main hall only to see the handcuffs gleaming in one policeman's hands. Several of them were trying to take Ray down to the floor. He was furious and fists were flying. Then the back of Ray's tuxedo split in two. That was it. We were done here. I said a quick goodbye to my unimpressed parents, and ran out the front door with Ray. By then, Sue was waiting in her Mercury Cougar with Phil.

A couple of policemen tried to block our exit. One opened Phil's car door, grabbed him and threw him into a snow bank. Little did they know he'd had a broken back in the past.

I watched in horror, hoping he was still able to move. The last hurrah was having Sue's passenger door torn nearly off her car by these boys. It was disgusting. Someone helped Phil up out of the snow and we all piled into the car and slid most of the way on icy roads to Sue's tiny one-bedroom home only a few miles away. Only once we were safe in Sue's house sitting down was I able to cry. I sobbed over the whole mess and the embarrassment of it all. Sue's dog, an overweight dachshund came and jumped up into my lap and nestled into my layers of wedding dress, looking up at me as if to say, "I understand." My night was complete.

Chapter 21

MAJOR MISSTEPS:
The Corvette
The Burn
The Surprise

Ray and I moved into an apartment in Waterford when we returned from our honeymoon in Niagara Falls. Niagara Falls in January had been a virtual ghost town. Many restaurants were closed, and the ones open only had a few customers. The roads were treacherous, and walking on portions of frozen waterfalls was not very exciting and disappointing at best. Yes, it was a poor choice for both of us. It should have been fun in the sun, tropical drinks, golf, and maybe even a moonlight swim or two. Then there was the auto repair bill for Sue's car door that was waiting for us, so we wrote a check from the wedding money we received. It was time to concentrate on getting settled and start cohabitation. I was determined to love Ray and make things work.

There were many auto workers laid off that first year and one day Ray spotted a yellow 1965 Corvette with a for sale sign in the car window. The auto worker couldn't keep up the payments or the insurance. Ray really wanted that car so we traded my 1965 Plymouth Belvedere, the Blue Funk and thirteen hundred dollars for it. It was pale yellow with a convertible and a hardtop, side pipes, baffles, and a four speed. I drove it much of the time, and being a policeman's wife, I didn't speed, but policemen would pull me over frequently. The conversation always was the same.

"I'd like your driver's license and registration, please. I bet you're wondering why I pulled you over. Uh, are you interested in selling this car?"

I'd be polite, and sweetly say no, but after it happened at least ten times, I began answering a question with a question, saying, "Do you see a for sale sign in the window?" It was maddening. Then there was the time a Michigan State Trooper passed four cars over the double yellow line to get behind me with lights and siren on, only to rifle through everything in my car stating he was "looking for drugs" and my car was on his drug list. He didn't ask if I wanted to sell the car – he was just plain rude. In fact, he was such an ass, I told Ray about him and his badge number and he made a phone call to the State Police post. In the next three years, the car would require engine work, several U-joints, and it received a fresh paint job out of state because of stress cracks. My Blue Funk wasn't half as much fun, but it was a much more affordable car.

The Burn

It was May of 1970 and I was anxious for summer to arrive. Ray was looking forward to playing a lot of golf and we had talked of joining a policemen's couples golf league. While Ray was on the afternoon shift, I was working days at the hospital, so we shared only a few nights having dinner together at home. We both enjoyed entertaining when he was off and had established a well stocked bar for our get-togethers. A beautiful set of bar glasses was featured in a catalog – clear glass with a lime green design and a line of gold around the rim and we ordered them for the bar. The day they arrived, Ray and I were home and excitedly unpacked them admiring the unique sizes and shapes of each glass. I set them on the kitchen counter so they could be washed up later with the dinner dishes.

I was somewhat of a novice cook. Mom didn't really want us in her kitchen underfoot because the home we grew up in had an extremely small kitchen area, even though Dad had built in a Lazy Susan and a pull out table. The most I knew about cooking was strictly observation, but baking was very easy for me. Mom had been a great cook and I wanted to be one, too. That particular day I was roasting a slab of ham and potatoes. Reaching into the oven to pull out the baking dish from the lower oven rack, my left forearm touched the upper rack. Instantly, my skin sizzled and stuck to it. As I yelped with pain and pulled back my arm, the skin tore off in one piece. The oven had won. I wasn't so lucky.

Ray yelled to me from the other room, "What's wrong?"

Running cool water over the fresh burn, I whimpered, "I just burned myself on the oven."

He strode into in the kitchen, glanced at my arm and scolding loudly said, "How could you be so stupid? That was so stupid of you, Beth, stupid and careless . . ." I was taken aback. His words stung as badly as the burn. I began to cry out loud, which only made things worse.

"Oh, you want to cry now, eh? Well, cry over this." I was standing barefoot in the kitchen and watched in disbelief as he grabbed the first of several of the new glasses off the counter and began smashing them to the floor. When he was through, there was glass encircling my bare feet and he marched out of the kitchen leaving me there trapped by the littering glass. Minutes passed before Ray returned to the kitchen, hoisted me into his arms, carried me out of the kitchen and roughly set me down onto the carpeting. He never apologized. I was frightened and wanted to run away. We had only been married four months and this behavior was not even believable. Was I truly stupid? Did he really think that about me? Was I the fool for putting up with this without going ballistic? Surely, this was to be my "light bulb moment." I had some serious thinking to do and it kept me awake all that night. The next day, I was driving on Walton Boulevard to the grocery store lost in thought over what to do when a driver pulled up next to me waving me over. I recognized the grin. It was Jimmy from high school days.

"Hey, stop over to my house, you remember where, don't you? Sarge would love to see you and I want you to see my new motorcycle."

"I can't Jimmy. I'm married now and Ray wouldn't like it. I just can't."

"Awe heck, we go way back . . . it's just a visit. Five minutes. What's the harm?"

I had just seen Ray's wrath a day earlier. I bowed my head, let out a long sigh and shook my head no. Then nervously, I looked in the rear view mirror to see if any police car was in sight.

"Hey, what's going on with you?" Jimmy said as he stared at me, sounding truly concerned.

"I have to go, Jimmy. Nice seeing you." I drove slowly away with tears flooding my eyes. I knew I should never be this unsettled and unhappy. I decided then and there that I needed to meet with my parents.

Another thing that was complicating our lives was sex. Before we married we had used condoms. I had never had sex with him without one on. But after we married I went on birth control pills.

The very first time we had sex minus the condom, I made a cruel discovery. His sperm burned my insides as if I were on fire. I left the bed, ran a tubful of bath water, sat in it and cried. We tried several times with the same results. Since Ray was the first and only man I had been intimate with, I had no idea what was normal and what wasn't. I just knew that this made sex a huge letdown. I made an appointment with my gynecologist.

"What is it, Doctor? The burning is so severe, I can hardly stand it. Is there something wrong with me?"

"I'm not sure, Beth. I don't know if it's an allergic reaction or what, but you are raw inside. If the only way you can be comfortable is with him using a condom, I suggest he use one. The lambskin condoms are thin and will give him more sensation and protect you."

So, we did. Now, any man will tell you he'd much rather have sex without wearing a condom, but I knew if Ray didn't, I would grow to hate having sex with him. It was miserable for both of us in different ways, but it was the only way and it remained that way for quite some time. I tried using a diaphragm after that. I truly wondered if other women went through this and whether I could ever enjoy sex without a condom or something else in the middle.

A few days after running into Jimmy and after a lot of soul searching, I called and made arrangements to meet with Mom and Dad while Ray was at work. I told Mom it was something serious and we needed to talk. When I got there, Mom shooed the kids outdoors and we sat in the dining room across the table from each other, Dad and Mom both looking intently at me. This was going to be awkward.

"Well, the reason I wanted to talk to you is that I need your advice. I think I've made a terrible mistake." Then I proceeded to explain about the recent burn and glass breaking incident, along with his need to know exactly where I was nearly every minute. I was even concerned he would be trying to track me down while I was at their house. I couldn't understand this distrust. Then there was silence. My father said nothing. Then my mother spoke.

"Beth, you made your bed and now you'll have to lie in it." That was all. I was frustrated and left feeling very alone.

Life went on. I left the job at the hospital and went to work for the cardiologists. Ray and I got to know our next door neighbor, Rene. He was a window designer/trimmer for a chain of men's clothing stores and Capitol Records. He was gray-haired, chewed his cigarettes like cigars, had been in the Merchant Marines, then married and divorced, and was now living in the apartment next door. He arrived home very late many nights and we knew exactly when because his refrigerator backed up to the headboard in our bedroom. You could count on two items being in his refrigerator: one hundred proof vodka and orange juice. The two bottles would clink together upon his arrival to the kitchen. Sometimes we'd pound hello on the wall. If we were still up, we'd go have a drink with him. His apartment was decorated like a festive bar in the Hawaiian Islands. He quickly became part of our circle of friends and even brought a classy redhead over from time to time that lived in our complex. We had plenty of company and had a lot of good times with others around. It was our times alone that put us to the test.

Then, Ray took a position working undercover with the police force. One day Ray went into a tirade over me taking too long getting home from work. He demanded to know if I was having an affair with one of the cardiologists, Dr. K, a kindly Greek doctor who had daughters my age. He backed me up against a wall, drew his fist back, and I instinctively shut my eyes. He struck the wall right next to my head with his fist and broke through the drywall. Pieces of it began to fall all over the floor. I was a wreck. After he left, I heard Rene rummaging around next door. I knocked on the wall with a broomstick and he knocked back. I felt he was like a lifeline that I needed. I called him and told him I needed to talk to someone. I went next door and told him about what Ray did, how crazy he was acting and that I didn't want to live like that.

"Beth, maybe it's the job or maybe it's something he'll have to outgrow. If not, then you'll know when you have to leave." We didn't talk about it again. At least he would know there was trouble if my knocking became frantic.

The Surprise

One day, Ray called me at work and said he had a surprise for me and to meet him at his parents' house after work. I had no clue what it would be. When I arrived, his blue Pontiac was in their driveway. There was no answer at the front door, so I walked around to the fenced in back yard. Ray spotted me walking toward him but I suddenly stopped in my tracks. My heart was pounding with fear. Ray was on one side of the yard and I was on the other. He had a large German shepherd by the collar. Frightening memories of being mauled by dogs came flooding back to me.

"This is Bruno! He's a police dog and I just bought him from a guy at work. He only understands German. He's really great and he's so smart. You're going to love him. Put that padded sleeve on. I'm going to have him attack so just hold your arm out in front of you."

"Ray, I don't want to . . . no . . . ," I said almost pleading.

"Oh, quit it and put the sleeve on. You better hurry because I'm letting him loose."

As Ray gave the attack command, I shook pulling the sleeve on my arm. The dog began charging across the yard toward me barking loudly. When he reached me he jumped up and clamped his teeth onto my padded arm. I was terrified.

"Isn't that something?" Ray said as he praised Bruno. Once he had a grip on the dog and I'd been "released," I pulled off the sleeve and stormed out of the yard.

"Hey, where are you going?"

"Away from that dog, that's where," I yelled back as I headed for the front porch.

Ray closed the fence gate and followed me trying to catch up.

"Ray, why would you ever buy a dog without talking to me about it? Don't I get any say in this? I would not be comfortable with that dog in case you didn't notice. We're living in an apartment that doesn't allow dogs, either. Where are you going to keep it? We don't have hardly any money saved. How much did you pay for it?"

"Only five hundred. I had enough for a down payment. We can keep him here at Mom and Dad's until we get into a house. I just have to go buy some dog food."

Someone wasn't listening, or was and didn't give a damn. I was fit to be tied. I didn't ask Ray's father how he felt about having to clean up dog dung in his yard when it wasn't even his dog. I figured that was between Ray and him. Not a week had passed when I got a phone call from Ray's dad.

"Beth, I need to get a hold of Ray about the dog. Bruno was chained in the back yard and jumped the fence. Beth, he hung himself. He's dead. I don't know what Ray will want to do."

So, for the next three months, we paid the policeman cash installments for a dead dog and I breathed a sigh of relief.

Chapter 22

THE SEPARATION

During the next six years, Ray and I rode the marriage roller coaster. We spent most of our leisure time playing cards and golf with our friends. Ray had gone from patrol officer to narcotics, then eventually took a position on the police department where he was able to work with citizens regarding safeguarding their homes and gave talks to neighborhood groups. We bought a tri-level home and got a dog, a yellow Labrador retriever, naming her Abigail, Duchess of Rowley or Abby for short. After I had worked five years for the cardiologists, I was summoned to Dr. K's office. I was concerned. He seemed happy with my work and could see that I took a sincere interest in patients and their symptoms. In fact, he had arranged for me to be allowed to round with the medical residents one day a week at St. Joseph Mercy Hospital so I could see our patients from the hospital side of things. I had looked forward to the educational stimulation of it and had gone on these rounds for several months. I knocked on his office door, and then went in.

"Beth, I wanted to talk to you. You've worked for me long enough for me to notice that you're extremely intelligent and I feel you're wasting yourself. I know you take my JAMA Magazine and read it nearly cover to cover every month and if medicine is such an interest to you, I think it's time for you to challenge yourself more. You should consider going to college now. If you want to try for medical school I'll help any way I can but at the very least, nursing school."

I was stunned at first, but very flattered. I could hardly wait to talk to Ray about it. As I drove home that day, I was so excited that someone had thought I was smart, smart enough for even medical school. After all, wasn't it time for me to do something for myself? For the last two years, Ray had been going to Michigan State to get his Master's Degree in Criminal Justice attending evening classes. I proofread and typed all of his assignments, and he even kidded that when he got his sheepskin from college he would owe me half of it. The only schooling I'd done was taking one college course in 1968, and Bishop Sewing classes from Bishop One through Bishop Six at night polishing my sewing techniques on everything from a simple apron to men's suits. But the nights I wanted to stay home and sew, Ray demanded I go ride to Michigan State with him and back, "because I don't trust you home alone. If you don't go, I'm not going either, and it'll be your fault if I don't finish." Some nights after the long ride there in blinding snow, I was told to stay in the car and wait for him. His brother, Mickey was attending college there fulltime and there were a handful of times I was "allowed" to go to his dorm room and wait there. It was embarrassing and degrading and I hated it. Still, I remained as the consummate peacekeeper. But I was ready to make my case on this night.

"Ray, Dr. K called me into the office today. He said he thinks I'm smart enough and with my ambition I should be considering college. He offered his help regarding information on nursing programs or even medical school. Now that you're almost done with school, I'd like to take my turn at it."

His stare was cold as ice. Without any hesitation, he stepped toward me and put his hands on his hips.

"No, Beth, you will not be going to college, not now, not ever because you'll meet someone else and you'll leave me…and we are never having this conversation again, do you understand?"

That was to be the end of it. I was furious with him for bullying me. Sadly, I shared his response with Dr. K and he was extremely disappointed. He had three daughters of his own and had always encouraged them to better themselves. Besides, Dr. K was not a big fan of Ray's. Months before, Ray had marched into my doctors' office waiting room one afternoon in full police uniform, took my arm and walked me out into the hallway which frightened the group of mostly older patients. They began asking the receptionist what I had done. In the hallway, he began to accuse me of sneaking off to the Machus Red Fox Restaurant and having a cozy lunch with "a doctor." I had never been there in my life and demanded to know who was telling him these things. It was one of his police buddies.

"Ray, I don't know why your 'buddy' is making this stuff up about me unless it's to get your goat, but he is. I'm sick of this.

Who should you believe—someone who's married to you, or one of your cop friends?"

"I believe him over you because he's the one watching my back."

The next day, Dr. K approached me and sternly said, "Beth, I do not want another scene in this office involving your husband coming in here like that and upsetting my patients. If he does, you'll be fired."

My face was beet-red and felt like it was on fire. I quietly slid into the restroom and stood in the dark until I could compose myself.

Before that, there were a couple of policemen's wives who had decided to take police courses at the community college and try to get on the same police force as their husbands. I mentioned it to Ray that I thought I'd make a decent policewoman and his response was "over my dead body." But this newest letdown did make me re-examine my job, and within a few months I gave my notice and decided to move on. I worked doing some free-lance billing and reorganizing for doctors' and lawyers' offices, and took temporary assignments as a Kelly Girl. I had felt the need to break out of this stagnation I was in.

An assignment at General Motors led to an interview with the owner of a small advertising agency. Dick's business was up above a women's clothing store in Bloomfield Hills. It was a small office where he, his father and a fellow named Tom worked fulltime, and Dick's wife would come in where she was needed and when they were swamped. The secretary/odd job/Jacqueline-of-all-trades position was available and soon it was offered to me.

There were times I was included in brainstorming sessions regarding new jingles for products or campaign slogans for the car industry. We had twenty-two Pontiac dealerships to service and got the contract for the prestigious Detroit Auto Show two years in a row. It was pretty amazing considering how small Market Response Group really was. But, the hours became crazy during crunch time and there were times I was at the office printing press releases and putting out written invitations until very late. Even though I let Ray know I'd be delayed, it was causing considerable tension between us and eventually we separated. There was only one earlier time it had come to a separation and I spent the night at

Ray's godmother's house until he sheepishly apologized for being so accusatory and asked me to come home. I felt that this time it was going to take some considerable effort to mend the divide between us. Ridiculous spats and relentless jealousy left me feeling smothered. I had just begun to get some self-confidence and I was determined to let myself breathe again. My sister, Robin and cousin, Gail were renting a house from my parents and I asked to rent the third bedroom. It wasn't long before I heard rumblings that Ray was spending private time with a hostess from a local upscale restaurant and her son. After all of Ray's unfounded accusations of me, I was steaming and told Tom, my coworker about it. Tom and I would stop for lunch together when returning from meetings or just to get out of the office. He was a wonderful friend. He'd talk about his wife and their life, both of them in advertising. Not a hint of distrust or accusatory conversations were mentioned. I wondered how this mess evolved in my marriage or whether it was just very common for cops' wives. The divorce rate among his cop buddies was incredibly high.

"Well, now that you know where this woman works, do you want to go over there?" Tom asked me. "Do you want me to go check her out?"

"Not just yet. I'm sure the opportunity will come. I'll wait. I can be a very patient person."

And it did come. Several weeks after we separated, Ray called and asked if he could take me to lunch to talk. I said I would go and when he asked what time to pick me up, I said, "I'll meet you at the Main Event," the restaurant where his new sweetie worked. "It's so close to my office," I explained.

I purposely arrived early. The hostess asked to take my name to get a reservation in.

"Table for two," and when she asked for the last name, I saw her cringe, then turn pale.

"I'm meeting my husband for lunch," I said with a forced smile. Ray arrived late as usual and appeared nervous. She glared at Ray while seating us.

In the meantime, my own boss seemed to be enjoying throwing men in my path, almost as if it was a game. One was encouraged by him to send me flowers and two dozen roses arrived. There were two and three martini business lunches where two, three or four of us would "do lunch" with clients. I grew to love a good martini but I was a lousy typist all afternoon; I knew it couldn't continue. I got invitations for after-work get-togethers which were just temptations.

One evening as I was just leaving work, my boss handed me two very expensive front row center tickets to see Diana Ross in concert in Detroit. The concert was in a few hours and having no one to go with I handed them back.

"Dick, I can't think of anyone to go with this late and I won't go alone down in Detroit. I appreciate it, but maybe you can find somebody else to use them."

"Take them. I can't use them tonight either," as he wrapped my hand around the tickets.

I knew they were probably a freebie. He'd been booking a lot of radio commercials and I figured they were a gift. I drove home and nobody was there. Robin was working and Gail was with her boyfriend. Then I remembered a former friend from high school was on the wait staff of a restaurant/nightclub just a few miles from where I was staying. I called Joyce at work and told her what I had and she said she'd ask around inside and to bring them over. I did and what happened next changed my life.

Chapter 23

THE DOOMSDAY DRINK:
The Hospital
The Earring and the Knife
The Visit

Since I had separated from Ray I avoided going to any bars; I wanted no hint of impropriety. When I arrived at The Inn Between, I walked down the corridor to the main room which contained the bar/restaurant. I was met by the bouncer, a stocky guy with dark hair.

"Hi, is Joyce busy? She's expecting me to drop off some tickets. My name's Beth."

"Sure, I'll tell her. Grab a seat over there."

"No thanks. I'll wait right here." The doorway was close enough for me.

"Hey, suit yourself," he said shrugging his shoulders. Joyce, a pretty blonde with big, blue eyes breezed by with a tray full of food and drinks and said she'd be right back. I stood and awkwardly fumbled with the tickets until she returned. Then I heard a familiar voice call out my name.

"Hey, Beth – over here—it's my birthday! Come on over and have a drink with us." It was my dentist, Jerry. Ray and I had become social friends of Jerry and his wife and we'd gone out for dinners and to their home as well. He was sitting at a large round table with his all-female office staff and one man I did not know. I knew most of the women at the table from being in his office and Jerry introduced the man as "Tom." My first thought was that I shouldn't be here in this bar even if it's with my dentist and his staff. There's always talk and I'll have to defend myself and my actions. But then I rationalized, what's the harm? I'll be polite, have a drink and leave. I told Jerry why I had stopped there just in case he talked to Ray. No harm, no foul. There was small talk going on at the table when I suddenly felt sick. The room became a blur.

"Jerry, I have to go. I'm not feeling well. I don't know what's happening." It wasn't the alcohol. It was something else, something

I'd never experienced. As I got up, I struggled to keep my balance. My heart was racing. The man at the table told Jerry he had to go, too.

"Hey, Tom, make sure she gets to her car okay, will you?" Jerry called out. I stopped outside and fished for my car keys but the blurred vision and dizziness didn't subside.

"Here let me help you," Tom said as he took my keys away, opened his passenger door and pushed me in. I drifted in and out of consciousness and then heard voices. He had driven up to a small building and was talking to a man who was standing outside of the car. The next thing I remembered was being pulled out of his vehicle and his arm around my waist literally lifting my feet off the ground as the toes of my black boots dragged across the concrete. I was being lifted through doorway and I watched as one of my large, pearl-colored earrings bounced slowly down some dark turquoise stairs in front of me, as if in slow motion. I remembered nothing more until I was lying down flat on my back and he was pulling my clothes off me. I felt entirely immobilized and began moaning when he got on top of me. It felt like the weight of him was crushing and making it hard for me to breathe. I was begging, "Please, please no – I'll get pregnant, no, no, no." I hadn't been on birth control since the separation. There was no reason to take it. I heard him say, "I'll take care of it if you do," and then he raped me. He was pushing up and down on me so hard; I was only able to get an occasional breath. Afterward, he rolled off me and I passed out.

Sometime later I woke up to hear him say, "I've got to get you out of here," and with that, he pulled my legs off the bed and onto the floor and stood me up. Then he pushed me into his shower and washed me off. I was barely conscious when I was redressed, and driven to the inn's parking lot. Hours must have passed. There were no other cars in the lot. He said nothing to me as he tugged on my arms and headed to my car, unlocked the door and pushed me into the front seat. Then he tossed the keys into my lap, closed the door and left me there in the icy cold of winter. I passed out again and awoke near daybreak and somehow drove the two miles to the house where I was staying, passing out again in the driveway. My sister, Robin found me there when she walked outside to get the morning newspaper.

The knock on my car window made me open my eyes. "What are you doing out here? What's wrong?" Robin asked.

"I'm sick. I need help. Help me into the house," I said weakly. I continued to feel my heart racing in my chest.

"I'm calling Mom," Robin declared. My parents lived next door. Mom came right over and sat on the sofa next to me.

"What's this about you feeling sick? Is it your gallbladder again? Should I call Dr. McPherson?"

I had been hospitalized a year earlier for a gallbladder attack. She called him and he said to take me to the emergency room. It could be another attack, he told her.

Yes, it was an attack, all right but not that kind. I just couldn't talk about it. I only wanted to shower and get the stench of him off me. It was then that I totally understood why women crave a shower after an experience like this. The shame of it is that it never erases anything except evidence; the memory lingers on and on. My lips were blue and my fingers and toes were white with frostbite. I could have frozen to death in my car. How could any civilized person leave me there with no regard to what might happen to me? It was hard for me to fathom.

I had to ease on the warm water. Frostbite stings terribly when anything but tepid water is used right away. I knew about it from suffering a terrible case of frostbite when I was fifteen. My sister and I were at a winter church retreat up north ice skating on a large lake with friends under the moonlight. After several hours, I sat down on the dock, slipped my left skate off and my foot dropped to the dock, bouncing off it like a rock. I was more cautious with the right foot, but the result was the same. My feet were frozen. Three of us were sent to the camp first aid nurse. She told us the treatment was to run around barefoot in the snow for as long as we could. I couldn't believe this had anything to do with scientific data. Then we had to go inside and stick our feet in water. It was incredibly painful. I spent the next 6 months with the skin on my toes turning gray, shriveling up and falling off only to expose light pink toes covered in new skin. It was similar to a snake shedding its skin. It was bizarre and was repeated at least two more times. Give me sun, sand, surf, anything but snow and bitter weather. To this day, I am not a winter girl.

My heart continued to race. After thawing out in the shower, my quilted pink robe was comforting all wrapped around me. Now my mind was numb to everything except for one huge issue; I was a policeman's wife going through a separation from a man with a very short fuse. I was drugged, abducted, raped, dumped back into a parking lot and left there in the middle of winter to freeze to death. All I could think about was that Ray would want to find this man and kill him and all of our struggles to get ahead and for him to get his Masters degree would all be for nothing. But what if I told him and he didn't believe me just like in the past? What if he did believe me and hunted this man down and ended up in prison for it? What if I was pregnant? I was so very torn on what to do.

I called my gynecologist and told him it was an emergency. I needed to see him. He didn't ask why. He just told me in I should go to Emergency. I couldn't go there. There were always cops roaming around. I changed it to urgent. It was urgent that I see him. I wasn't able to be seen until the following day. My heart was still racing, but not as fast. There were no rape crisis centers then and little sympathy for women entangled in these kinds of messes. The prevailing attitude, "she probably asked for it" was more the tone.

When I got to the office the following day, my doctor was very empathetic to my dilemma and my concerns with Ray being a policeman. I had bruises surfacing on my abdomen, pelvis and upper thighs. I felt so ashamed, not at myself but at the gravity of the situation I had brought into his office. He was gentle doing his examination. I studied his face—it was so somber. I wondered how many women had come to his office after being raped.

"I'm afraid I'll have to put you in the hospital. You're pretty torn up inside, "and with that I began to cry.

"Doctor, what should I do about this? I'm so afraid of what Ray will do and I would be blamed for everything."

"I think you're gut reaction is right, but you'll have to do what seems right to you, not him. I do think that if you're fearful of how this will end, I wouldn't tell him now."

The doctor told me he'd wait until morning to call Ray and he assured me he would respect the doctor-patient confidentiality and keep things between us. The following morning I was wheeled into the pre-op area. I heard Ray's voice as he walked toward the gurney.

"So, what landed you in here? Your doctor told me it's some female trouble."

"Yes, Ray – it is. I'm really tired. I didn't get much sleep last night. Sorry I don't feel like talking right now."

I was terribly depressed and I wanted him to leave before I asked God to just let me die right there and right then. That's all. Then I went into a deep sleep.

When I awoke, it was over. I was in the recovery room. The doctor came by and quietly said it went fine and that I wasn't pregnant, a great relief to me. I feebly squeezed his arm and said thank you.

"Do you want to see your husband now?" He's in the waiting room."

"Just for a few minutes. I'm still woozy and I might say the wrong thing. I don't need him getting suspicious of anything."

"Beth, know one thing—I won't send you home unless it's to your house where your husband can look after you. The man that did this to you might get scared and do something stupid. I think you should have some protection around you."

I was wheeled out of the hospital the following day. Ray was taking me home. I stayed until the next day but felt panicky just being around him. I couldn't risk letting my guard down. I was afraid I'd slip up somehow and all hell would break loose. I left while he was at work and went back to my rented room. I couldn't risk him seeing all the bruising and the vacant look in my eyes. I had looked in the mirror and it was as if nobody was there.

Three days later, I was angry, really angry at the whole terrible episode. I didn't know at the time that I was going through something similar to the stages of grieving, just like when you lose someone you love. Looking back, I was in the anger and resentment stage. I decided I had to find out who this man was, where he took me, and why he did it. I felt it was an apartment of some type, but where? I got a map and circled a ten mile radius of the Inn Between. Within that space, I started calling complexes pretending I was a potential renter. I began methodically visiting them one by one, asking about whether there were stairs and carpeting colors. Recalling the dark turquoise stairs I was dragged

85

down, they were my best lead. Lucky number seven—the seventh complex I visited had a guard shack near the entrance. Maybe that's who this man spoke to when we drove in. So, I was disappointed when I asked the manager about carpeting.

"Yes, I'd like a little color in my apartment. What color carpeting do you use here?"

"Oh, beige. It's nice and neutral and goes with everything. Will that work? You look disappointed."

"I am. I was hoping you'd say a dark color like turquoise or dark blue or something."

"Oh, I totally forgot. We still have two buildings where the new carpeting hasn't been installed yet. And yes, it's dark turquoise and one unit's vacant. That should make you happy. Would you like to see it?"

My heart was beating so loudly in my ears I barely heard him. My mouth was bone dry.

"Sounds like it might work. Can I see it now?"

"Sure, the hallway doors are usually unlocked until dark. Somebody always leaves without locking up. I've got another appointment coming any minute. Do you mind going over and looking by yourself? It's a unit on the second floor in that first building right there. Here's the key. I'll be right here when you're through."

My hands were trembling as I took the key. As I entered the building I noticed a short stairway that headed downward straight ahead of me. Slowly descending the stairs, I ended up on a landing in front of an apartment door. The stairway was cut out underneath and it was there that I found my big, pearlescent earring. There was no doubt; I was in the right place.

I returned to the house and my rented room. I had to go back and confront this man. I was sorry I couldn't go to my own kitchen. I had a boning knife there with a five inch blade, my favorite knife to use for everything. I needed one to hide in my purse. I settled for a steak knife with a serrated blade. Just in case he came at me, I was determined he would not hurt me ever again. I decided to get back to that one apartment on the lower level and wait for my attacker.

No one was around when I entered the apartment building. I cautiously crept down the stairs and tucked myself under the staircase. I took my earring I had found out of a side pants pocket and stared at it while my mind wandered. He had been a little careless.

Hours went by before the outer door opened and someone started down the stairs. It was the man. It was Tom. My heart began racing again. I could hardly speak but mustered the courage while he slid his key into the door knob. I quietly reached into my purse and used my fingers to search for the knife. I held it firmly in my left hand as I stood up. He was totally taken by surprise.

"I want some information from you now. Just walk in. I'm right here," I said coldly as I let him see the knife. As we entered his apartment, there was a look of bewilderment on his face.

"What do you want? What's the knife for?" as he began to squirm.

"I want to know why you drugged my drink and why you raped me. How could you ever do that?"

"I didn't drug your drink. I think I know who did . . . I just took advantage of it." His voice had gone up an octave and he was talking very fast while he looked at the knife.

"I just got out of the hospital because of you. I had to have surgery because of what you did to me. What do you think would be fair?" I snarled at him.

He began to whine like a baby. "Please don't hurt me," he said looking at me pleadingly.

The irony of it...here stands this big man begging just like I begged him before he raped me. Now he wants me not to hurt him – amazing. I was cold as stone staring at him. After a long, long pause, I'd made up my mind.

"You know, you're not worth me going to prison for hurting you, you worthless piece of shit. You're not worth anything. You're just scum." Then I left.

A few weeks later, Ray and I reconciled and decided to look for some property and build a new house and start over. We sold the 1965 Corvette and used the money for a lot in a nice subdivision. He said he would stop seeing his "friend," the hostess. I began going to school in the evening to get my real estate license and to leave the advertising life behind. It was time. We never discussed my hospitalization and I didn't tell him what happened to me. But,

I couldn't have him lie on top of me, not anytime soon. I knew I'd panic and he wouldn't understand.

Chapter 24

REAL ESTATE SCHOOL

As Ray and I began paying visits to our new vacant property we met a few of our future neighbors. Patsy and Bob lived two lots down. Bob was a builder and he and his wife owned a Realty World office in what was known then as "Drayton Plains," now part of Waterford. Patsy was enthusiastic about the real estate business and offered me a position in their office when I obtained my license. We had several jack pine trees to remove from the build site, so Ray and I got busy using my father's chain saw felling trees and cutting them up to save ourselves money. On my days off, I'd go alone and work cutting wood for several hours. I corded the wood as I progressed and was relieved when it was finished. A few days later, we pulled in and noticed someone had stolen every bit of the wood.

Real estate school was held in a building off Telegraph Road near Twelve Mile. I worked at the ad agency and then drove to evening classes. I didn't tell my boss what my plans were. I wanted to pass my Real Estate Boards first before giving my notice. I was pretty disillusioned with him anyway because he made promises of a company car, gas card and the like, none of which materialized. Instead, we were relocating to larger and more expensive digs and he was decorating his office walls with suede. Suede? I knew it was time for me to go.

Another future neighbor was also attending real estate school and I'd see her at class. Candy and her husband were having a house built and would be living across the street from us. She also had aspirations of working for Realty World. The day before the State Board exam, we agreed to ride together to Lansing for the test. The following morning, I was up and ready before she was to pick me up. She had said she knew her way around Lansing. I did not. It was a long drive and I was anxious to get going. Being nervous about passing the exam, I barely slept. More time passed and no sign of her. I began calling her house with no answer. The third time, a sleepy voice said, "Hello?"

"Candy, what are you doing? Do you know what time it is? We should have left twenty minutes ago!" I said, frazzled. Once the doors are closed for the exam, no one is allowed in. Then the trip would all be for nothing, and we'd both have to wait for it to be offered again.

"Oh, gosh, oh gosh, I'll be there in five minutes," and she was, thrown together, but there.

She drove a racy Firebird and we literally flew to Lansing. I know she was driving over a hundred miles an hour a few times. We cruised up and down streets looking for the address, then parked and raced into the building about fifteen seconds before they closed the doors. Forget having time to get psyched for the test. It was now or never. Afterward, they announced your name if you passed, and we both did. We were ecstatic and drove to meet several others at a pub for a celebratory drink. On the way home, we missed an expressway turn and ended up at Detroit Metropolitan Airport an hour out of our way, but we were both still happy just the same.

Chapter 25

WINNING TWO TRIPS, KEEPING HALF

After my real estate career got off the ground, my confidence began to flourish again. Our house was finished and we moved in. It was a very interesting custom built ranch with a sunken music room and a raised dining area with an oak floor that would double as a dance floor for parties. Ray and I didn't really bicker as many couples do when building a new house. We both seemed quietly content for the most part, but there was still something unsettling, an underlying current cutting through our lives. One morning, while thumbing through classifieds, we spotted a job opportunity which required moving to Saudi Arabia for two years. The job was a security position and the pay was great. Living arrangements were to be in a compound with British, German and French employees. If Ray had written the ad himself, he couldn't have fit the position any better. I figured if we went, maybe I could find a medical position over there. Ray had complained daily for some time that he was not happy at the police department. We had only lived in our home for a few months, but he called his parents to see if they would be willing to move in and watch the house while we were gone if he got the job. His younger sister, Kathy was still in school and would be able to stay in the same school system. We met with them and got the go-ahead to leave – they would stay at our house since they were in a rental themselves. So, Ray said he applied for the position. My thinking on the subject was if we went and had only ourselves to rely on, it would bring us closer together. Maybe we could even have a baby while we were gone. Then, I began to count the days waiting to hear something from this overseas company.

At the real estate office, contests were held for the most listings in a month, the most sales volume in a month, and most build jobs sold. If one of our customers seemed too hard to please when looking at existing homes, we'd turn them on to building a brand new home of their own. One month I was awarded a trip for two to Las Vegas for selling build jobs. I was excited to tell Ray we could go to Las Vegas on someone else's dime. There were others from the office going at the same time. It would really be fun. He came home that afternoon and I surprised him with the news.

"Ray, I've got tickets for two for Las Vegas all paid for. I won them for selling build jobs. Are you ready to have some fun in the sun?"

"I don't think I want to go. No . . . I don't," he muttered.

"But, why won't you go? We need to get away, just you and me. We haven't heard a thing from the Saudi's about that job for you. So, let's take a break and go, okay?"

"Yeah, I guess. Okay, I'll go."

"Good." And then over the course of the next several weeks, Ray changed his mind about every other day. As the departure day drew closer and he came home saying he wasn't going again, I blew up.

"Listen, I've asked you to please go with me on this trip. I don't ask for much, you know. It's important to me. We need some time away to talk about our future. If you think our marriage is important I believe you'll go because it is to me. I'm fed up with you constantly changing your mind. If you won't go on this trip with me, I'm filing for divorce when I get home. "

He said nothing more about the trip, pro or con. I just wanted to know if he was going to back out. Then, about a week before the trip he strolled in from work to make his announcement.

"Oh, I thought I'd let you know—I'm not going to Las Vegas with you after all and I sold my half of the trip."

"You did what? You 'sold' your half? It wasn't yours to sell. I won it. What did you get for it?"

"Three hundred dollars."

"So, I'll have a "roommate in MY hotel room?" I said lividly. "Where did this bright idea come from?"

"A cop I work with . . . his wife, Joanie wanted to go so she'll be taking my place," he said with a smirk.

"Remember what I said, Ray," as I walked out of the house and took a walk. I was shaking and angry as hell at him.

The morning the airport shuttle bus pulled into the driveway, he carried my suitcase to the van. I don't recall a kiss, just "I'll see you when you get back." Then he walked back into the house. On the plane, it was hard to keep from crying . . . for myself and for Ray. I had sacrificed my skating career, was held back from attending college, and mistrusted constantly. He was going to miss me, I told myself. There was a tremendous heaviness in my chest. It didn't subside and a couple from my office sitting across the aisle was concerned. He had a bad heart and carried nitroglycerin with him always. His wife asked if I wanted to take one.

"No thanks. I just need to get off this plane and go someplace quiet to think."

They checked into the hotel and it turned out we were on the same hallway. When the pain didn't let up, I knocked on their door and said I'd try the nitroglycerin. Then I lied down in the dark until my roommate arrived dressed like a cowgirl wearing boots and a bandana tied around her neck. Joanie was very sweet. I just wasn't in the mood for extending social graces considering the circumstances. Once the nitroglycerin kicked in, I began suffering from one of the the worst headaches I'd had in my life. Joanie was all excited and could hardly wait to go to the casino. I wanted none of it. I stayed in the room that night and most of the next day revisiting the memories of the last eight years. Then, I had an epiphany.

He's not ruining this whole trip for me. I refuse to let him, I thought. I got in the shower and washed the saltiness off my face, did my hair, and got out my favorite maroon jumpsuit and heels. I was going to survive this deadness I felt. I had read about shooting craps and wanted to try the game. I watched a table for several minutes and stepped forward to bet. Eventually, the dice came to me. After several rolls, I was still in the game. Several more rolls and people were starting to cheer. Then, suddenly many people began betting against me except for three men at the table. I got in several more rolls before crapping out. I had barely bet on myself. These three men were beaming and approached me as I left the table.

"Where did you learn to roll dice like that?" one asked. I explained that it was just beginner's luck, that I'd never played the game before. Another said, "Do you have any idea how much money we just made off you?" I blushed and said I didn't have a clue.

"Well, what are you doing for the next couple of days? Would you roll dice for us?" I was flattered and said "yes" since I didn't want to be alone the whole trip and it would give me something to do. The three of them were there for a swimming pool convention for two more days and then were heading back to their home town, Albuquerque, New Mexico. I'd never been out west except for Vegas. Besides a few hours of solitary sleep, we stayed together in a group for those two days. I felt like queen of the prom. One man, Glenn was charming and flirtatious. The other two just made me laugh. When they asked why I was there alone I told them the truth. My husband wasn't interested in being with me and sold his half of my hotel room to someone I'd never even met and his actions pushed me over the edge. I was going to file for divorce when I got home. There, I'd said it out loud and I meant it.

The third day I was there, I ran into people from my office who said, "Somebody's been paging you overhead in the casinos." I hadn't paid any attention and hadn't heard it until that afternoon. I went to the house phone. It was Ray.

"I decided to come out there, okay?"

"Well, that's just fine except you'll have to find yourself a hotel room. The other half of mine is already occupied, remember?"

"Never mind, then!" he snapped and hung up on me.

The last thing my new-found friends said was that they had so much fun, they wanted me to be able to visit New Mexico sometime so they chipped in with their winnings and bought me a first class round trip ticket there and back from Detroit. I was impressed but not exactly sure I believed it. People say a lot of things in Vegas. I was dreading the trip back to Michigan, but it was nice living in fantasyland, even if only for a few days. Joanie was adjusting nicely to having free rein. She was upbeat and cheerful every time I ran into her. I wondered if Ray had rekindled things with the hostess while I was gone.

The flight back was much quieter than the trip there. Most people were asleep on the plane. I was wondering what type of reception I would get returning home. The shuttle bus delivered me to my door. As I walked in, there was a lit candle burning next to a bud vase with a single red rose in it. Too late, I thought, and it was too late.

Chapter 26

MOVING OUT – THE PIANO STAYS

The next several days at home were very quiet. I had no idea who to call for legal advice. My parents suggested I call my Uncle Bob, who was a lawyer turned politician, first becoming a U.S. Congressman, then a U.S. Senator. In fact, my sisters and I stomped the campaign trail with him one summer day visiting campsites and small towns. He recommended an attorney, Mr. S. He was a pleasant young man and my wish was to settle this divorce peaceably. Since there seemed to be no malice regarding our breakup, he suggested we both use him as our attorney. Later, that decision turned out not to be such a good idea.

The week I was to file in the fall of 1976, we were still living under the same roof but I slept in the guest room. It was undecided where I was going to live. However, that week something happened that determined for me that anywhere was safer than staying. It was very late when Ray came home after work one night. I wasn't able to sleep and was lying on my side facing away from the door. I heard him pour himself a drink at the bar. The ice was making a tinkling noise inside his glass. He was later than usual that night and I wondered if he had stopped with his cop friends at a bar on his way home. I heard him walk up toward the bedroom door which was open. I held very still. I wanted no conversation or angry words erupting. I hoped that he would think I was asleep. Then I heard a snap. The only thing with a snap on it was his holster. Did he take out his gun? Was he pointing it at me?

"If I can't have you, nobody else will," he said barely audible, with no emotion whatsoever.

I held my breath and stayed motionless. I was afraid if I made a sudden move, it might startle him and he would pull the trigger. I couldn't look at him. All I could think of were the patients at the hospital in intensive care for gunshot wounds, paralyzed. I thought if he fired, it would rip through my back and not kill me, just maim me. Then, who would ever want me.

Seconds seemed like minutes. I'd never been so still. The silence was deafening until I heard him slide the gun back into his holster and walk back down the hallway with drink in hand. It was frightening. I decided then it would be my last night in our house. I moved out the next day taking only my clothes, landing back at my parents' rental house next door to their home. The used piano, a 1918 Wheelock five foot grand we had just purchased months earlier would have to stay put for now. The next day, I cancelled my piano lessons at Clarkston Conservatory of Music. It was a shame; I was just getting excited about playing again.

There was one thing that troubled me and it was the trip overseas. Would that have helped mend our broken marriage? I would have been willing to try. I didn't want to be another divorcee. It really bothered me so I just came out with it.

"I wanted to ask you, Ray – did you hear anything about the job in Saudi Arabia? Did they ever contact you?"

It became just another disappointment as the lie surfaced. And without even a glance my way he answered sullenly.

"I never applied."

Chapter 27

THE SUICIDE SCARE

It was a pretty typical day at the real estate office. I was making cold calls and working on a listing presentation. There had been some rumors going around the office that Ray had recently moved a young woman into our home. Since the divorce decree was a ways off, it was a bit insulting. My neighbors became aware as the news drifted through the area like black smoke.

In the afternoon a call was transferred to me. It was Ray out of control.

"I just wanted you to know, I'm going to kill myself and you know that I can. I have the guns to do it. I want to see you. I need to talk to you and not over the phone . . . in person or I'll do it, I will."

"Ray you're just talking foolish. Whatever has you upset like this, you should be calling the Department psychologist, not me. You've been in contact with him. Let him know you need to talk to him."

I had also met the Police Department psychologist. After he had seen Ray earlier that month, he asked if I would be willing to meet with him so he could get a better picture of what he was dealing with. We agreed to meet at an office in a local hospital. I went there during his lunch hour. He had packed himself a sandwich and gave me half. We spent about thirty minutes together when he offered me his observation.

"Well, you are not the major cause of his problems."

Ray told me after my meeting with the psychologist, a comment was made to Ray that took him by surprise.

"Do you know what he said to me, Beth? He said that I was the nicest son of a bitch he had ever met. What do you make of that?" he sputtered.

I reflected on that statement while I now had him on the phone ranting. Then it escalated.

"No, no, I need you to see me now, today, or I'll do it, I mean it." He was starting to sound scary and very unstable. His voice was shaky and higher pitched, not the low "I'm in control" voice I was used to hearing. I was torn. I didn't want to step into a situation that could possibly lead to a murder/suicide if he went off on me. But, if I was the one who could talk him down and didn't, then was that wrong? How would I feel if he did kill himself? What had suddenly gotten him so distraught? He wouldn't say.

"Okay, I'll be over in a few minutes," I uttered reluctantly and quickly hung up the phone. I walked out to the front office to talk to the secretary and one of the other agents.

"Listen, my husband is home threatening to kill himself. Call this number—it's the police psychologist and tell him I'm on my way over there. If I don't call you within ten minutes, call the police and tell them to come right away." I had no idea what I was walking into.

It was a dreary overcast day. As I pulled into our driveway, I decided I was going to wait outside by my car. I didn't want to be ambushed. Cautiously looking toward the house, the garage door suddenly rose up about two and a half feet and Ray rolled out from under it, and then jumped to his feet. There was no gun in sight. I stepped out of my car, but left the door open.

"What is going on with you, Ray? What's wrong?"

A moment later, a young woman with long dark hair swung open the front door and glared at me. Ray looked over at her.

"See . . . told you Beth just won't leave me alone! So, now do you believe me?"

My mouth literally dropped open in disbelief. I got back into my car. The car engine roared as I pulled away from the house and out of the neighborhood. I made it back to the office before ten minutes had even passed. Peggy, our secretary looking concerned, asking me what happened.

"Oh, it was just another attempt to jerk my chain. I feel so stupid for believing him." I slammed the bathroom door behind me and stared into the mirror. It didn't say "chump" on my forehead. "What a foolish, gullible woman you are," my image seemed to say back. Then the psychologist called on the phone concerned and wanting to know why Ray wasn't answering the phone.

"Because he was busy playing me for a fool in front of his girlfriend," I answered tersely. "Never again – he's all yours," I said with an air of finality. The psychologist thanked me and hung up.

Two hours passed, and the second call from Ray was routed through to me. It was the same threat. He sounded distraught again. I wasn't buying it and told him to call his psychologist and hung up on him. Then I walked out and told Peggy I was leaving the office for the day. No more phone calls, please. My nerves couldn't take it. Tomorrow would be a new day.

Chapter 28

SUPER BOWL SUNDAY'S NOT SO SUPER

On the day of the 1978 Super Bowl XII in Louisiana, I was at my office putting together a picture board of a new listing. My old neighbors threw a big party on that day. Since Ray still lived in the neighborhood, he got the invite. I had just finished up at the office and was heading out the back door to return to my temporary home when the phone rang. Ray was on the other end.

"Beth, there's something important I have to talk to you about and it can't wait."

"It sounds like you're at a party, Ray. What is it?" I asked disdainfully.

"It's not something I can talk to you about over the phone. I need to see you."

I was not the least bit interested in getting pulled into some psycho-drama. Maybe it was the booze. He wasn't slurring his words. I had no idea.

"Why is it so important right now, today, Ray?"

"Because it is, Beth. You'll want to know what I've decided, believe me."

Was it some kind of trap? Only Ray knew that. I hesitated and then said, "The only way I'll meet you anywhere is if it's in a public place."

"Okay, okay, fine. Where do you want to meet? "

We settled on Oceania Inn, a Chinese restaurant on Dixie Highway. It was a busy street and the parking lot was wide open for anyone to see. I knew they'd be open for business, too.
Twenty minutes later, we were sitting face to face in a high-back booth. I just stared at him.

"I've been doing a lot of thinking. I want you to come back and get pregnant with my child. After you have the baby, you give me total custody and don't see it again, ever. In return, I'll give you the house, furniture, everything."

I wanted to explode. "Do you think I've waited all these years to have a baby and would just hand it over to you? For a house? For furniture? Are you kidding me? No, Ray, I won't "sell" you a baby! I cannot believe you'd stoop to this." I stormed out of the restaurant, got in the car and locked the doors. He didn't follow me and I was relieved. This new twist scared me.

A few weeks later, I ran into an auto salesman that we both knew and he was at the Super Bowl party when Ray returned from meeting me at the restaurant that day. His next statement was unbelievable.

"So did you think you could talk Ray into swapping your house for a baby? He told the people at the party that now he knew you were nuts."

He also said that Ray told them the entire meeting was my idea – so much for giving him time to tear the truth to shreds. Little did I know he was trying to lay more important ground work. Our final court date was rapidly approaching in February. I was determined to bring this mess to a close. No more meetings with him. He'd have to address me through "our" attorney. I should have guessed he was on to his next stratagem.

Chapter 29

MENTAL INCOMPETENCE

During the course of the upcoming weeks, I never knew what to expect. What did was the furthest thing from my mind. I was served papers that I was to appear in court for a competency hearing. How embarrassing and humiliating this turned out to be. Ray had gotten a judge who was a drinking buddy of the police to sign the order. Well, they must have sat in a bar dreaming this one up. Ray was claiming that I was not in my right mind and certainly couldn't be trusted to make a decision such as divorce in my present mental state. Ray wanted to have me committed to a mental institution, Pontiac State Hospital, for evaluation and treatment if necessary. I was dumbfounded.

My day in court, the divorce lawyer accompanied me. I knew he'd have to stay in my corner from that day on. There would never be another episode of "lawyer-sharing" in my lifetime. I was called upon to take a seat up in front of the courtroom. There were lots of people seated as observers. I would be one of those observers later in my life.

"State your name and your address, please."

It was very formal. Scanning the audience, I didn't think this would help my real estate career a lick. I answered the next few questions matter-of-factly.

"What is your occupation?"

"I'm a realtor. I list and sell homes and vacant land."

"And how many days a week do you spend doing real estate?"

"Seven right now. I'm working very hard at building a new career for myself."

There were a few remaining questions and then the judge spoke, stating he could see no reason to have me declared incompetent. Case dismissed. Ray crossed over the line with this stunt trying to find ways to delay our divorce from being finalized. However, he did succeed in getting it postponed for over a month. What a way to buy time.

Chapter 30

GRANDMA IS MY ROOMMATE

On March 17, 1978, the day of the divorce, I knew I was the only one who needed to show up for court. Yet, when I arrived, Ray was there and spotted me in the corridor. I disappeared into a stairway and quickly opted for climbing the stairs. Suddenly, Ray started down and met me on the landing. I just held my breath.

"I know you're not going to go through with this. You know you won't. In fact, I'm so sure I brought Jeff and Nan with me." Jeff was our builder and Nan was his wife. We had spent time together with them having dinner, barhopping and on a recent fishing trip.

"Jeff and I will be waiting for both of you at Kennedy's Pub. Nan's going to be in the courtroom. I told her to give you a ride over and then we'll all celebrate." He was unbelievable.

When my case was called and I was put on the stand sworn to tell the truth, it was Judge Gilbert who began to question me. She asked if there was any chance that the two of us would ever consider reconciliation. I began to stammer, and said if things hadn't been so conflicted   possibly things would have turned out differently. All I could think of was the times people had asked me why I had stayed with Ray so long with his jealousy and distrust of me, and my answer was always, "Because I thought he'd outgrow it and he never did."

Suddenly, Judge Gilbert made a comment that I didn't seem to be sure about what I wanted and she had a notion to deny the divorce. I glanced out into the people in the courtroom and locked eyes with Nan who was staring at me. I mumbled something about that wouldn't solve anything and yes, I wanted the divorce.

The divorce was granted. Nan went to Kennedy's alone and broke the news. It was official.

I drove to Al's house, a realtor who had been my mentor in the office. He was very sweet and had been understanding and kind during those months I had worked with him. We would take one day off from real estate every two to three weeks and go to the movies midday and cook burgers on his twelve-inch hibachi. I collapsed on his sofa, pulled my wedding ring off, and fell asleep. Court had turned out to be really stressful. I was so relieved it was over.

My grandmother on my father's side had been staying in Florida through the winter. She and my granddad had a condo in Boynton Beach. Beulah and Julius loved their place there, right on the Intercostals Waterway. Granddad died unexpectedly at age seventy-three after suffering a heart attack while staying at their Michigan cottage. He was hospitalized, but the myocardial infarction wasn't detected until it was too late. Grandma had decided to continue going to Florida after his death. She didn't drive, so a family member would fly down with her and get her settled in late fall, and someone would fly down in the spring and bring her back. Since the cottage had been sold, Grandma would become my roommate for about six months. We actually enjoyed each other's company a lot and usually had breakfast together in the morning.

Grandma and I had a very unusual and special connection. I swear it was telepathic. While she was staying in Florida and I was at my office, I suddenly got this intense feeling something was amiss with her. I immediately called her in Florida and asked her if something was wrong. She was so present in my mind.

"Oh, I'm so glad you got my message."

"Did you leave me a message here with the secretary?"

"Oh, no . . . you know what I mean . . . that 'thing' we do. I'm very sick and I wondered if you could come and get me."

"Of course I will. I'll be on the first flight I can book. I should see you tonight."

"Oh, thank you, honey."

I flew down to Florida that night, rented a car and drove immediately to the condo. Her color was very pale and she was having a lot of pain in her abdomen. Grandma had been treated at least ten years earlier for cancer of the uterus and intestinal area and had tolerated an ileostomy ever since. We flew back to Michigan the next day. In the meantime, my credit card company was trying to hunt me down because of the "suspicious activity" with my card mainly because of two trip bookings in two days. Grandma was taken into the hospital the day after our return. She had adhesions from her previous surgeries and one of her kidneys was affected, but she pulled through another surgery with flying colors.

Even though I was working long hours at the office especially on weekends, I wanted an outlet other than going to the bar when business got tough. Many of the real estate agents I worked with would try to recruit others to hit the bar when they were having a bad day or a bad week—the more people crying in their beer, the better it seemed and the adage, "misery loves company" certainly seemed to be true. I was determined to deal with my disappointment in some other way. So, I joined Arthur Murray Dance Studio and became a pretty good dancer. I loved disco dancing and many of the members would go out together after lessons just to dance our legs off. When I was having a discouraging day at work, I'd tell Peggy, the secretary, "I'm going to go dance for a couple of hours. Be back later." It was much better for the waistline than booze. I'd return renewed, refreshed, and sober.

I'd occasionally go clubbing with a co-worker. One evening, a very handsome guy named Ralph asked me to dance and we barely stopped the rest of the evening. He was easy to follow on the dance floor, fun, and he wore great cologne. He lived in an apartment nearby, was self-sufficient working in his parents' business, but was quirky in that he couldn't fall asleep unless disco music was playing all night in the background. A huge character flaw surfaced –he didn't trust women to be honest or loyal and I was included. However, I didn't know it until a "problem" came up that involved my family and lost me my temporary home with Grandma.

I had gone to bed late one evening, dead tired. My new friend, Ralph was supposedly out of town. A man dressed in dark clothing walked around the back of our house and was peering in the windows. My maternal grandfather was living next door with his new wife. It was about two a.m. Their dog began to bark; Grandpa got up and looked outdoors, and then approached this man while pointing a loaded shotgun at him.

"What are you doing out here?" Grandpa asked him.

"I'm looking to see who Beth's screwing in there," he answered. Grandpa chased him off. It had been raining and it was extremely muddy behind the house. I slept through the whole thing.

The next morning, my folks called and asked me to come over right away. Dad started out.

"Grandpa said he chased someone off last night, someone who was looking in the bedroom windows of your house. The guy told Grandpa he wanted to see who you were sleeping with in not so nice terms. Now, you know we don't approve of that kind of thing and your grandmother shouldn't have to put up with it either." Then it was Mom's turn.

"Your dad and I have decided that you should move out so Grandma can have some peace."

I couldn't believe it. I walked around the back of the house and there were muddy footprints everywhere, especially underneath the bedroom windows. That night, Ralph called and said he was back in town and asked if I wanted to get together. I told him I'd stop over. When I got there, a pair of his black leather shoes was sitting on a newspaper by the front door. They were covered in mud.

"Were you at my house last night?'

"Of course not – I told you I was out of town."

"Well, then explain to me how your shoes got so muddy, will you?"

Ralph grinned. "I just thought I'd check up on you and see if you were fooling around."

"Well, my friend, you just got me evicted from the house. I hope your curiosity was worth it. You know, I cannot believe you would say what you did to my grandfather. You have no class. Do not, I repeat, do not ever call me again."

I called Al to see if he knew of any rental properties I could possibly rent. He said the upper unit of duplex he owned with our broker was empty. It was only a few miles from the office. I took it and moved that week after I apologized to Grandma for my former friend's bad behavior. Then I went and saw Grandpa and thanked him for showing me what a jerk this guy turned out to be.

The day before I moved, I was driving to work down Elizabeth Lake Road when a car pulled into the inside lane and stayed beside me. I sped up and the other car did too. When I slowed down to thirty miles an hour and the other car did too, I glanced over at the driver. It was my rapist, grinning at me. I immediately pulled off the road near the entrance of Pontiac

Country Club and vomited. I had no idea his image would have such a sickening effect on me.

Chapter 31

BUILDING AGAIN

After Mom and Dad had gotten past being upset with my former male acquaintance and his peeping Tom antics, life seemed to be getting back to normal. No one had been caught peering in Grandma's bedroom windows since I moved. My challenge on the other hand, was dealing with the neighbors living down below me at the duplex. The cigarette smoke wafted into my apartment day and night along with the odor of burnt popcorn. How many times can you burn popcorn before you learn? Then, there were the verbal fights going on several times a week with screaming and yelling at all hours. I was getting to work tired and crabby. My parents had built a new home and two of my sisters and their husbands had recently, too. One day I got a surprise from the folks.

"Beth, your dad and I were wondering if you'd be interested in buying the forty-foot lot we own that runs off Morningside? You might want to consider building yourself a house, too."

It was part of their property with their previous house on Cooley Lake Road, but when they sold and built another off a side street, they decided to keep the lot for awhile instead of selling it with the house. I grew excited at the concept. I never thought I'd be able to build another house anytime soon. I met with Bob, the builder and came up with a house plan for a small two bedroom that I could afford. I was twenty-eight years old and counting the days until moving day.

Before the house was finished, I was contacted to come into the bank to sign off on the final builder's draw. I wasn't very comfortable with that seeing that I did not have a working gas meter on my house or a functioning heating system. I was told I had to sign off anyway. I was not at all happy with this and couldn't believe it. It was the only time I was sorry that I didn't have an attorney with me; I had given him a pre-closing package to check over my documents and give his blessing prior to closing. That first winter in my new home, I nearly froze when sitting in my living room. It was as if no furnace heat was reaching there. After discussing it with various people, there was only one thing left to do; go down into the crawl space and investigate.

In the spring, I removed the crawl space door and headed in. The crawl space itself was so low, (barely two and a half cinder block deep) that it was impossible to even turn over while in there. My claustrophobia was surfacing. It was very dark at first when I entered the space through the back of the house. I crawled in on my belly and waited a few moments until my eyes adjusted to the darkness. There, not five inches away from my face was a very big nest of black snakes and I was heading right into them. I don't remember a time in my entire life that I was able to move so quickly. Using only my feet, I back-pedaled and was out of there in less than five seconds. I was that spooked. A decision was made that very minute that I would never ever again enter the crawl space when I was there alone.

My next trip in and with a brother standing by, I was armed with firecrackers, a shovel, and a bright flashlight. There was a huge pile of dirt blocking my view, so I began digging the pile down and spreading the dirt outward. Near the back of the crawl space I saw the heating problem. The duct work was not even connected and I had only been heating the crawl space all winter! Lesson learned: always do your own inspections even if your township inspectors give their seal of approval. No one will pay your bills for you, no matter how unhappy or cold you might be. Also, snakes no matter what kind, still turn my stomach.

Another issue that I felt needed addressing was my piano. I had been nervous about leaving it with Ray because it looked great in our home and he knew it, but he didn't play at all. So, in May of 1978 I requested a letter from him saying that it did belong to me free and clear of any claims later. He had one drafted by an attorney friend of his and I had my copy, so I thought there were no worries. After I had gotten settled in my new house, I was ready to bring music back into my life and move the piano in, but Ray refused to let me have it. I never dreamed he would take me to court over it, but he did. I produced the letter in court, the judge ruled in my favor and it was over. A few days later, I made arrangements with Ray to allow me to come over with Bob, a friend of mine who was also my piano tuner and move the piano to my place. When we arrived, Ray said, "I'm going for a jog–try not to be here when I get back."

So, here was my piano, my 1918 Wheelock five foot grand sitting there like a lonely child. I had really missed her. Music at times was my salvation. This was my baby. My heart sunk when I got a better look. Ray had taken silver duct tape and stuck it across the lid like ribbon on a present. There was a two-inch square yellow paper smack in the middle under the tape. My friend was miffed. He had originally found me the piano and had done all the work to restore it.

"Now why did he have to put the damn tape all over the top? Beth, it's going to ruin the wood finish taking it off. What a mess."

"That's probably the point. He lost in court, so I have to pay. It's so childish."

We tried removing the tape slowly and gently, but it did remove some of the finish off the wood and in other places the sticky adhesive remained. After taking the tape off, the little yellow note was still there. I unfolded it. On paper from a yellow legal pad it simply said,

"I'll be moving to Indiana, but nowhere on this earth will be far enough away from you."

How nice. Bob and I had just gotten the piano out the door by moving it on a piano board and were loading it onto a truck bed when the "jogger" returned. I contained my anger, got into the truck and we drove away. There was nothing civil left to say.

Chapter 32

A TUMBLE AND NEAR TRAGEDY

It seemed like an ordinary day at the office. I received a call from a woman who wanted to see a house in Indian Village in Pontiac. We met at the house. I was wearing a soft peach-colored dress and heels when I met my potential customer in the driveway of the brick two-story home. The minute we entered, it had the feel of my grandparents' place where they previously lived and it was probably built by the same builder. The attractive black woman was dressed in a crisp, white uniform and said she had just finished her nursing shift at a local hospital. The upstairs landing was covered in large-looped green shag carpeting. While she walked down the stairs from the bedrooms and in to see the living room, I checked to see if any lights had been left on upstairs. As I took my first step off the landing, I felt a tug on my leg. It seemed my high heel had gotten caught in one of the carpet loops. I began to tumble forward down the stairs.

"Oh, my God!" The woman shrieked as I hit the floor. I was embarrassed to death.

"Are you okay? What a fall you took!" she said offering me a hand up. I was a site. My nylons were in shreds at the knees but nothing was bruised more than my ego. I stood up brushing my dress back down into place.

"First fall this year!" I exclaimed, thinking a little humor might help. "So, what do you think of the house?"

"Hmmm, I need to think this one over."

Normally, I would have used one of the soft closings I had learned in my sales class, but instead said, "Alright, I'll call you tomorrow."

I looked over my knees once I was in the car. I had rug burns on both of them and a very sore back.

Fifteen minutes later while heading down Dixie Highway back to the office, traffic came to a screeching halt. There was a small boy with blond tousled hair lying on the pavement in front of my Oldsmobile. He had just been struck by a car in oncoming traffic and had literally been knocked right out of his little red tennis shoes into my lane. One of the shoes was stuck under the front wheel of a car driven by a large, black woman.

"I didn't mean to – didn't see him. He ran right out in the street!" she screamed. She had such fear in her eyes I felt sorry for her.

I ran to the boy who looked to be about five or six. He was bleeding profusely from the head. I remembered something a paramedic had once told me. "If you see blood squirting out of somebody, stop it with anything you got." I felt under the side of his head resting on the pavement where the blood was pooling. I could feel the pulsating blood hitting my fingers. There was a large dent in his skull. He began to squirm, wanting to get up. I talked softly to him and held my fingers tightly to his head, cradling it in my lap. I flashed back to taking care of my little brothers when they were hurt, but nothing this badly. Moments later another boy maybe eleven or twelve appeared in the street. Traffic was stopped in every lane.

"Oh no, oh no, he got hit, didn't he? He was following me. I told him not to. Oh, my mom's going to be so mad," he said staring at the blood. The little boy was barely conscious.

"Is this your little brother?"

"Yeah." he said, as he started to cry.

"Hon, go get your mother right away. There's an ambulance coming. They'll need her here. Run fast, okay? I'll stay here with your brother."

Pretty soon, a young woman ran up saying she was an off-duty paramedic and she stayed close by. Then the ambulance crew arrived and she told them to grab an I.V. and some pressure dressings. I held his head, motioning to where the bleeding was coming from. The paramedics gently lifted the boy off me and they were loading the stretcher into the truck when his frantic mother arrived.

"Thank you," she said tearfully as she climbed into the back with her little boy. It was over. Traffic started to drive around my parked car. Funny, here I was in front of the Oceania Inn, the same restaurant where Ray and I met on that one Super Bowl Sunday. A kind, Chinese man came out and asked if he could get me anything. I said, "A towel would be nice." My hands and forearms were covered in sticky blood as was the front of my dress.

He came back out with a large starched red napkin. It wouldn't remove a thing.

"Thanks, that's okay. My office is close by. I'll wash up there."

I got back into my car to drive the rest of the way back to the office which was about a mile. As I pulled away from the accident scene, my legs suddenly started knocking together. It was like an aftershock. I pulled to the back of the real estate office and got out of the car. My legs were still quivering. When I opened the office door, another realtor named Stacy was sitting at his desk. He glanced up at me, surveyed my bloody arms and my dress, and then looked down to my skinned knees and torn nylons.

"Wow, rough appointment," he said and went right back to writing and never asked me a thing.

"Yeah, you could say that," I whispered, choking out the words.

Later, I found out from the police the boy's name and called the hospital. I was able to talk to his mother who said he sustained a fractured skull. He left the hospital in three weeks. I was happy for him and for his older brother. His brother probably was the one who had the nightmares just like I did when I nearly lost my brother through the ice. It stays with you a long time.

Chapter 33

A CHANCE MEETING WITH MOM – TWICE

In the fall of 1979, a chance meeting took place between my mother and one of my former classmates, Greg. Mom was Township Clerk, an elected position in Waterford. Greg was there trying to obtain information regarding licensing for a new business he wanted to open. He had been living up north for some time working as disc jockey at a pizzeria. Somewhere along the line he partnered up with another man named Tom to try and get this business off the ground.

"So, Mrs. Griffin, what's Beth doing now? Is she married or have any kids?"

"Well, Beth's in real estate. Her marriage ended recently, but she's doing well for herself."

"I'd really like to call her and say hello. Can I get her number from you?"

Mom gave it to him. Our families were friends. I had attended school with Greg and his brothers ever since fourth grade and through to my senior year in high school. Greg was good looking and a charmer with a perfect smile. He was from a blended family after his mother remarried someone with several children of his own. Greg had never shown any interest in me whatsoever until our fifth year class reunion and I was there with my husband Ray. He talked to me for several minutes there and that was it, so I was surprised when the phone rang and it was him. We agreed to meet for a drink locally, had a comfortable evening and said our goodbyes. He had been very curious about how I was getting along, how I was doing in real estate, and where I was living. I was impressed that he took an interest. He was looking to open a nightclub for teens in our area, and Mom's office was in the same township building where he was checking zoning requirements and permits.

It didn't take long before he was staying later and later at my house. His apartment was close by and he shared it with a young man named Mark that he brought with him from up north to work for him. Mark was a friendly but somewhat passive person that treated Greg like an idol.

Real estate was slowing to a crawl as it does nearing winter, but at the same time the Country was suffering from quickly escalating interest rates during the Carter administration. The very last house I sold that year was to a young man who was soon to pay an interest rate of eighteen and a half percent. It was jaw dropping. I was so glad I had built my home during better times. I left my real estate office and moved to another Realty World office on the outskirts of Waterford after a falling out with my broker, Steve. It was over a small real estate commission on a garage converted to a one-bedroom house and he wanted me to split the sale with a part time realtor in my office. I felt it was unfair. I was bullheaded and some sarcasm on his part led to my leaving.

I knew after selling real estate for a few years that November and December were very quiet months. I wanted to get into the Christmas spirit, so I took a part time position with J.L. Hudson's in the men's cologne and leather glove section of the store. I'd always been attracted to men that wear cologne and it was really pleasant having different scents swirling in the air. The rich smell of good leather emanating from the glove case was such a turn-on. It brought back memories of necking in a parked car with a young man wearing a sumptuous suede winter coat, suede gloves, and terrific cologne. I loved it for the atmosphere, but hated the continual standing just waiting for customers. I developed a new admiration of those wonderful store clerks that go through it day after day. My feet were killing me. I bought kinder shoes that first week.

In the meantime, Greg and his partner got the approval and licensing to open a nightclub for teens which would be open for age thirteen to nineteen year olds. They made arrangements to rent a large vacant storefront site which faced M-59 two miles from my house. I would stop up periodically to say hello as they bustled about transforming this lackluster space into an inviting showplace with a huge dance floor and colorful synchronized lighting on some of the walls. Greg and I began sleeping together regularly at my home, much to the chagrin of Mom who showed her wrath early one morning. Greg's blue truck was parked in my driveway when Mom pulled in behind him, stopping on her way to work. She jumped out of her car and marched up to us.

"It's pretty obvious that you two spent the night together and you know I don't approve of it. I can't believe that you have no shame. What'll people think of you? You're embarrassing me doing this in front of our neighbors!"

Even my being twenty-nine years old didn't make Mom any less upset with me. Greg and I just stared at each other as Mom huffed back to her car. We'd only been dating for a few months. This was the downside of living just a stone's throw from the folks—the privacy factor was non-existent. After she left, we talked about it. Somehow, the conversation came around to, "Let's just get married."

The club called "Spanky's Nightclub for Teens" was due to open in late December. We talked about getting married in January, about three weeks after the club opening. More bathrooms to put in, all new carpet and tile, tables and chairs, snack machines, building a D.J. booth and coat check room, and getting some video games together was the plan. Also, radio and newspaper advertising was going to be necessary to get a healthy crowd there opening night. Greg had some sound equipment, the furniture in his apartment and the blue stake truck which I believed was leased. I had been stopping in regularly to see if I could help in any way. Greg sent me to run errands while he and his small crew worked like dogs to get the remodeling and renovation done. It was an exciting and yet scary time to open a new business with the country in a recession. All the activity at the building was attracting many people, curious about this new place getting ready to open. Finally, there would be something different and special for teens to do.

Chapter 34

THE BUSINESS/MARRIAGE MIX

The club opening took place in December of 1979 the weekend before New Year's Eve and went really well except for one big problem that infuriated the business owners nearby. Apparently the plumber who plumbed the new bathrooms and set everything up forgot to remove the plug in the sewer line, and all the toilets began to back up in no time. It's got to be one of the worst nightmares for a business opening. It was chaotic. That night we had to relax the rule about "once you leave, you'll have to pay to get back in." There were kids coming and going, using the neighboring restaurant's bathrooms. The fallout was horrible and it instantly cast negativity on the club from opening night. It was winter and I don't know if anyone checked on emergency port-a-johns, but we could have used a half dozen. As it was, it was too little too late. I was in charge of internal security in the girls' bathrooms, and helping with coat check. Greg was the D.J. for the Friday and Saturday night dances. The sound system was awesome. He really understood what it took and tweaked the sound so it was not ear-deafening loud, but that the vibration of the beat could easily be felt. By the New Year's Eve party, all the perplexing problems had been ironed out. We increased our number of internal and external security people as the number of those attending rose.

I let my real estate broker, Bill know that I would probably be leaving the office after closing on my last sale. Real estate had slowed to nearly nothing with the interest rates inching into the low twenty's. Here was this new teen nightclub business defying the odds. Kids needed someplace to go that they could call their own, and Spanky's was that place.

We looked at engagement rings in December but Greg didn't have the money to spend at the time. We ended up buying them at J.L. Hudson, used my employee discount, and I paid for them, with him pitching in later. With both of us at age twenty-nine, Greg and I got married on January 20, 1980 at Spanky's, ten years and three days after my first marriage to Ray. Friends of mine from real estate, Jim and Linda were in attendance with our families. We left Mark and Tom in charge while we took a four-day cruise to the Bahamas. The cabin floor space was about the size of a postage stamp and totally uncomfortable with two bunk beds bolted to the wall. We pulled the mattresses down onto the floor and slept there the entire trip. Greg moved into my house once we were back, leaving most of his belongings except for his clothes at the apartment which Mark kept.

On January 11, 1980, I received the money owed me from the sale of Ray's and my home, over thirteen thousand dollars. After Greg and I returned from our honeymoon, business picked up each week. I did notice, though, that he was letting certain women into the club and up into his D.J. booth in spite of his own rule that no one except the D.J. was to be in there during the dances. With all of the equipment to attend to, it was just too distracting. He had even installed a lock from the inside. When I'd call him in the booth asking who his female friends were, he'd say, "Oh, it's just biz."

In February, there was the big Valentine's Day Dance to plan. Greg was outside our home when the mailman came. He walked out to get the stack of mail and then disappeared behind the house. That was very unusual. Later, I found the stack thrown on a makeshift workbench. There was an envelope addressed to him that he had opened. It was a Valentine's card from a woman. It seemed unbelievable that we were just married, he had lived with me for less than a month and another woman was sending Valentine's cards to him at my house. So who's giving out our address? The traffic in his D.J. booth also picked up as the club became more popular. One Friday night, a teenage girl stormed up to me outside the girl's bathroom.

"I hate your guts for you taking him away from me. I'd like to run you down with my car, you bitch. You know, I've been to his apartment. I can tell you what's in his bedroom, too. He's got a statue in there on his dresser where he hangs his jewelry. I've seen everything."

She was right. She definitely had been there and she was underage. Why had she been to his apartment? I'd only been there twice myself. That wasn't the first incident of this kind. A week

124

after our honeymoon, we were at the club in the middle of the day going over some things, when I answered a call.

"Put that son of a bitch on the f____ing phone, do you hear me?" a young woman screamed. She wouldn't give her name. I transferred the call to Greg and told him I didn't have a clue what it was about. He took the call up in the D.J. booth. They talked for several minutes while he paced back and forth. After he hung up, I called the booth.

"What was that all about? Who was that? Do you know how she talked to me?"

"Oh, she's just somebody that thinks I owe her some money for some equipment I have. Listen, she'll just be a nuisance, so just make out a check to her."

"What do you mean a nuisance? How much money do you owe her?"

"About three hundred, I guess. Yeah, make it out for three hundred."

"So, issue her a check from the Spanky's account?"

"No, make it a personal check."

Well, there was no way I was doing that. She sounded like a nut case. I took three hundred dollars out of my account and bought a money order. He told me her name and address and I mailed it. Several days later, she called again.

"Oh, you think you're so f____ing smart, don't you, sending me a money order. You haven't heard the last from me, you bitch!" The thrill of being a newlywed was quickly losing its luster. I would find out later, much later that this person had been dating Greg and knew nothing about us getting married until she saw our wedding announcement in the paper.

Things seemed to settle down after a bit. Greg wanted to build a garage behind the house. I had to constantly dig into my personal savings, paying for building supplies. That summer we finished it, laying the roof shingles on a very hot Memorial Day weekend. Greg also wanted to have an alarm system installed which we did. His brother, Jeff made a trip up from Texas and helped Greg pour a concrete driveway which took more dips into my savings. When I was selling real estate, I had bought a few homes and used them for rental properties. One by one, I sold out my interest to give us more liquidity. I bought a Plymouth Horizon stick shift in

February 1980 and Greg bought a van and customized it. Within a month of getting the garage finished, Greg and his partner, Tom decided to make some design changes at the club. Suddenly our garage became a staging and storage unit where all the building and assembly took place. There was no room for a car. So much for having a garage to use for vehicles.

Chapter 35

A STRIKE TO THE HEART

I thought we made a great team, Greg and I. We began having exercise classes several evenings a week at the club on the dance floor. Women seemed to enjoy the spacious room, the lights, and the sound system, all of it. It was great fun. We hired an instructor named Kathy who had incredible energy and charisma besides being very limber. I began participating until one day Greg suggested I do the D.J. work for the classes. It freed him up to do other things and it was a new skill I was happy to learn. Greg was upset that I had not added his name to my home, so that was done in February of 1981. Wall partitions were installed at the club to close off the exercise classes from the video arcade filled with video games. We had begun leasing and purchasing a diversified selection of video equipment and games causing the neighboring arcades to feel the competitive pinch. Later, a video token war ensued and kids were constantly going from place to place requesting larger amounts of tokens for a dollar.

In May, Tom talked to Greg about selling out his portion of the business and said he was going to move to Arizona. Since Tom was leaving, a new form of security deposit had to be placed with the landlord, so a lien was placed on my new car for seven thousand dollars. The payout to Tom was over thirty thousand dollars total for four thousand shares of Sundown Disco stock with twenty-five thousand of it paid out on June 12, 1981 at my attorney's firm with one of his associates handling the legal work. The remainder was due for payment in October of 1981. Many nights Greg was at the club very late keeping the game room open until midnight and then he'd stay and have drinks with the guys. It wasn't uncommon for him to come home at two or three in the morning at times. Then, one night everything changed.

It was about four a.m. and I was sound asleep. I suddenly awoke with such severe pain it took my breath away. Greg was sitting on top of me slamming his fist into my chest. I tried to speak and he hit me again and said, "I hate you, you c__t. I just couldn't do it on my own. I had to have your help. I really hate you for that."

I pushed him off me and he fell backwards off the bed. I ran for the back door of the house, frantically trying to unlock the deadbolt, when he grabbed my throat and shoved me back up against the door, never letting go of me.

"Where you off to, Babycakes? Wanna run away, is that it? Gonna cry now, huh?"

"Let go of me, Greg, let go. Why are you doing this?" I asked tearfully, my voice barely a whisper.

"Cuz I feel like it, that's why. What are you gonna do about it, huh? Hit me back?" he asked laughing.

I could barely breathe. The more I tried to move, the tighter he squeezed my throat. He began to sway unsteadily on his feet, and then fell to the floor. I scrambled out the door, running down the street in my nightclothes. When I got to my parents' house, I began pounding on the front door. I was afraid he might be close behind. Dad came to the door and let me in.

"What's wrong? What's happened?"

"I don't know, I don't know. He just hit me in the chest. I don't know why. I don't know what's happening. Why does he want to hurt me? What is wrong with him?" I asked as I stood shaking. Dad just shook his head.

"Thanks for letting me in, Dad."

"Where is he now?"

"I think he passed out. He fell and was lying on the floor when I ran out. I was afraid he'd come after me."

I was awake the rest of the night with my chest aching each time I took a breath. Hurt turned to anger by the next morning. I called the house and left him a message on the answering machine.

"Greg, after what happened last night, I'm going away for the weekend. I want you gone when I get back, understand? You're moving out."

I waited until I was sure he'd left the house in the morning. Mom drove me back home. I was wearing her blue robe as I walked up the back steps to use the emergency set of door keys I had left with her back when I had the house built. It was a somber moment walking back into our house. The answering machine message had been erased. I packed a suitcase, got in my car, and began to drive north. I was nearly to the Zilwaukee Bridge when I called Anne and Curly, Al's parents in Bay City.

"Come see us, Betsy. We'll be waiting for you."

I was relieved they were home. I didn't know where to go or what to do. I just knew that no one was going to use me for a punching bag ever again.

When I approached their front door and knocked, I heard a gruff barking from inside. I expected hunting dogs to be around as they always were, but I got a shock when the door opened. Standing next to Anne was a large red Doberman Pincher. It was the first one I'd ever been close to since I was a girl and was chewed on. The dog watched me closely as I edged my way past her. Anne and Curly welcomed me with open arms as I knew they would. I was devastated and broke down sitting in the familiar kitchen. I knew I needed to think this through before going home. The dog never left my side the entire visit; she even slept on the floor next to my bed. I grew to adore that dog – she was my ally.

I left Al's parents' place on Sunday and headed toward home, but knew when I crossed into Waterford I wasn't ready. I spent the night in a cheap motel seven miles from home. It will be better coming home on Monday, I told myself. He'll have payroll and banking to do from the weekend so he'll be busy. When I arrived at the house Monday morning, he was gone. Most of his clothes were removed from the closet and drawers. It was a relief.

I went to see my lawyer, David. He intently listened to my situation.

"I want a legal separation, David. I'm not going to take this. He could have killed me."

"Beth, there's no such thing as a legal separation in Michigan. You are either pending divorce or you're not. So, you have a choice; do nothing or file for divorce. That's your recourse." I checked on an annulment, but was told it wasn't feasible since we owned a property and a business together.

"Look at me, married for less than two years and facing another divorce. How did I ever get myself in this mess? What am I going to do for work, David? I can't go into the club and be anywhere near him right now because of what he did to me, but all my work revolves around that club, too."

The phones were ringing and ringing in the background. David got up and walked over, closing the door the rest of the way.

"Sorry for the distraction. Our receptionist quit. We really need someone out there. Listen, I know this would be different for you, but if you're willing, I'll check with the other attorneys and see if we can have you fill in at the front desk for the time being. It would give you some income and we can do your legal work without it costing you. What do you think?"

I was ready for anything. I knew I'd feel fairly safe there. He wouldn't mess with me while I was sitting in the middle of a group of attorneys.

"I'll do it if everyone's in agreement. When can you let me know?"

"Give me a couple of minutes." He strode out of his office as if on a mission.

David came back shortly and said it was approved and everything was going to be alright. I told him I needed some time before filing for divorce. I didn't want to be a two-time loser, but I didn't want to end up dead, either. The chest pain had subsided, but not the pain in my heart.

Chapter 36

ONE LAST CHANCE

In the late summer of 1981, I turned into the receptionist and biller for my attorney's office. I liked the secretaries there and each attorney had a different persona which kept things interesting. Greg and I remained separated. He had moved back into the apartment he once had shared with Mark, our manager. I began to breathe easier. Several of us would go to the local bar-restaurant on Wednesdays, "hump day" and it was nice to get to know everyone outside of the office.

I had noticed that in doing the billing that many of the accounts were uncollected. I was surprised at how many people didn't follow through paying their attorney fees. Since I had done all of Dr. K's billing for nearly five years and was very successful in collecting outstanding amounts, I felt that it should be possible to increase the rate of return for the attorneys. I was positive I could increase the percentage of their collection rate so I proposed a plan that would pay me a flat percentage of the amount instead of a salary if they would turn the task over to me, even on a trial basis to prove my worth and that I was right. The thought of increasing the amount of their income and my own as well seemed to make them squeamish and the idea was eventually rejected by the group. I felt defeated and returned to the role of receptionist and biller only.

The months passed and I was growing inpatient being in limbo with my marriage. Then one day, a dozen red roses were delivered to the office. They were from Greg with a card that said, "Let's talk. Love, Greg." I had been so embarrassed and ashamed about the incident that caused us to separate. I should have called the police, but it was humiliating and degrading to admit that someone you love felt so justified in beating on you. I'm sure that's why no one in my family asked why I didn't call the police that night. Also, Greg had become very friendly with some of the local police. Once they had become pals with him, I had no confidence they would take me seriously. I had known Greg over twenty years. I saw no signs. I didn't know why he wanted to hurt me. I went over what he had said to me that night a thousand times in my mind and still didn't understand. We agreed to meet and talk.

"Why did you hit me while I was sound asleep, Greg? Did you think I had done something that gave you a reason to smash your fist into my chest? It hurt for weeks. You could have killed me."

"No, if what I was trying to do was kill you, I would have. I just got drunk, that's all. I don't even remember much. I want to come back home and be with you. I'm sorry I hurt you. I'll never do anything like that again. Give me another chance."

"That's right; you won't because if you ever hit me again, I'll kill you. I mean it."

I couldn't believe that came out of my mouth, but at the time I was stone serious. Looking back, it sounded completely absurd.

The weeks before, I had been sewing to pass the time and keep my mind off the situation, but decided for some crazy reason to make Greg a velour long sleeved shirt. I never knew if I'd ever give it to him, even as a going away or should I say a "get lost" present. It would probably fit one of my brothers I thought. The night we decided to reconcile, I handed it to him on a hanger. We'd only been married a year and a half when we separated. Maybe I made it as a gesture of love doing something that I do best. Just one last chance and that would be all. I'd be able to walk away then, no matter how embarrassing it all turned out to be.

Chapter 37

MOVING ON UP AND MAYBE TO BEAUTY COLLEGE

Winter had arrived and after cautious consideration, I left my stint at the attorneys' office and returned to re-visit my marriage and start back to work at Spanky's. I told David, my attorney that I was willing to give Greg a second chance, but not a third. No one discouraged me and I thought I was doing the decent thing.

We had great success with the New Years Eve Dance, ringing in 1982. I was back doing the books, handling phone calls from parents and their inquiries, supervising the coat check and maintaining security in the restrooms. Within only a few months of being back together, Greg made an announcement while we were having a quiet dinner together.

"I think now that things are working out, we should look for another house, something with some more space."

It hadn't really occurred to me because I wanted to ease back into our relationship, not jump into quicksand. We had talked about having a child together, too. Within a week, he was coming home talking about this house or that house. The search had begun. A home right on Elizabeth Lake came on the market not a half mile away. It belonged to a large family like our own families. The outside structure was very sound, but the inside of the home was in extremely poor shape, about thirty-six hundred square feet including the walkout to the lake. We bought it anyway on a land contract paying twelve percent interest on April Fool's Day, 1982. Greg was very handy and I wasn't afraid of work either. The living room floor sloped steeply toward the middle like a funnel, so the first thing needed was to remove all of the carpeting and pour yards of concrete there to level it. The floor contained nonfunctioning radiant heating pipes in the existing concrete. The home was built with steel girders, probably leftover building supplies used by the original owner. With the concrete separating the floors, the house was virtually soundproofed.

Our manager, Mark moved into my smaller home and began to pay rent. On April 2, 1982, Greg ordered over twenty-two thousand dollars in video screens to be installed at Spanky's by a video center in Royal Oak. Eighteen days later, our new home was used as collateral for a twenty thousand dollar loan for equipment.

The first night we slept at the new house we were awakened by the noise of something large scurrying about in the attic right above our heads. In fact, it sounded like a foot race up there. The only inside access was in the kitchen. The following day armed with a flashlight and a broomstick, we opened the access. Nestled up above were two very large raccoons, their beady eyes staring back at us. I'd read that they don't like the smell of mothballs, so we bought a large box, opened the access and began throwing handfuls of them up into the darkness. They made a sound like marbles rolling everywhere. Moments later a large paw became visible.

"I can't believe it . . . they're throwing them back at us!" Greg yelled. We both began to laugh hysterically standing in the kitchen. It was the first time I'd laughed in months. We hurled more up there and they'd hurl them right back down at us. It truly was a laughable moment. That week, we hunted for their mystery route to the attic, and nailed the opening shut while the raccoons were out for the evening. Very early the next morning, we were awakened to a screeching sound coming down the chimney flue. They sounded really angry. It kept up for several nights with the piles of raccoon feces accumulating on the roof of the house. Eventually, they left for better living arrangements.

In June of 1982, Greg arranged for a thirty thousand dollar loan from his mother and step-father to be paid over three years. Then, in late November we would purchase nearly fifty video games for the game room costing almost one hundred fourteen thousand dollars, to be paid back in two thousand dollar weekly payments.

Our Spanky's landlord let us know that another building next to ours was going to be vacant within about a year. Greg was thinking of opening a second business next door to the first one, hoping that it would evolve into a business that would complement Spanky's. We talked about some options including a beauty salon for teens. It would have to be hip and flashy. Once we delved into the idea, we discovered that in order to manage a salon, you had to be a licensed cosmetologist. Greg and I talked about it, mulling over the idea that I could go to beauty college during the day and still be able to help out at the club at night and on the weekends. He emphatically said that he wanted the new business in his name and that I could "manage" the salon. I said no—that this marriage was going to be a partnership and if that wasn't how he felt, the deal was off. After some grumbling, he agreed to the business being in both our names.

We bought a used pontoon boat to be able to get out on the lake. I had been having cramping and just felt lousy in general. Then I missed two periods in a row. I decided one day when Greg and I were relaxing on the boat, I'd mention it to him and see how he'd feel about the possibility of fatherhood.

"Greg, remember when we talked about having a baby someday? Well, I've missed a couple of periods and have been feeling kind of crummy. I'm wondering if I might be pregnant."

"Tell you what, Beth. They have clinics to take care of that and I suggest you find one. We don't need that right now."

I was crestfallen at his response and became very quiet. The news threw him into a bad mood. I called and made a doctor's appointment when we came off the lake that day. It was hard to know whether to be sad or relieved when I saw the doctor days later.

"Well, you've got a large cyst on your ovary. It'll most likely burst on its own. I'm sorry if you're disappointed it's not a baby on the way."

"Me disappointed? Only at my husband—he didn't want it anyway."

Chapter 38

THE "BREAKDOWN"

In January of 1983, Greg and I took a quick trip to Las Vegas before I started Cosmetology School at Michigan College of Beauty. It would be our last relaxing getaway. His temperament changed after we returned. I climbed into our van with him on our way to run some errands, and as I set a can of Coke down in the cup holder, it tilted to one side. I reached into the holder and pulled out a pair of women's silver earrings for pierced ears.

"Greg, where did these come from? Whose are they?"

"They're yours, you know they are. Don't pull that crap on me!"

"No they're not, Greg. They're for pierced ears. I don't have pierced ears."

"Get the hell off my back, will you? Can't you think of anything else to bug me about? No other woman has been in this van. They're yours and you know it!"

I quietly removed them from the cup holder and put them in my pocket. Later, I moved them to a private place for safe keeping. I wanted to know who left them there. He had bought himself a very large set of drums and had them set up in our guest room. Greg didn't play, but his brother, Jeff did. Greg had suddenly decided he needed to learn to play. He was having severe mood swings and would sometimes play them for hours non-stop. He bought himself a gun, a nine millimeter with a shoulder holster. He said he needed it to carry when he made bank deposits. He sold his van and got a black Cadillac Eldorado. Then, one day things came to a screeching halt. He came home mid-day sullen and looking worn down, with dark circles under his eyes.

"I have to get away . . . need to go away. I want to drive down to Florida and lay around on the beach and not have to think." He was choking up. "Will you go to AAA and get me some maps to Florida? I want to leave today."

Was this a nervous breakdown? I'd never seen him act so desperate. Was this why he seemed so distant and moody? Maybe this push to expand the club and pay for all of the loans was starting to overwhelm him. I drove to AAA for the maps while he packed. When I returned, he was almost giddy, telling me he had talked to a business buddy, Jim, who suggested he fly to Hawaii the "second week." I frowned. How long was he planning on being gone? By sunset, he took the maps and was gone. I was left still attending beauty college during the day, getting to the club in the evening, and having to do all of the bank deposits and accounting. Mark handled the staff and security. Six days passed and I hadn't heard one word from Greg. He had taken his gun with him. I had become very concerned and drove over to see his mother and stepfather. When I arrived, the response was very different than what I anticipated.

"Why don't you just leave him alone!" his mother scolded. I had no idea where this was coming from.

"I thought maybe he was having a nervous breakdown. He wasn't in a good frame of mind when he left. I'm worried about him, that's all. I haven't heard a word from him."

I had no idea why she reacted that way. We had always gotten along very well. In fact, when Greg and I had moved into our house on the lake, she came over and helped me paint. She wouldn't say whether she had talked to him or not. I left their house confused and discouraged. Then the next evening, my sister, Terry called. We made small talk for a minute or two and then she told me why she had phoned.

"Well, I saw the kidney specialist today and he said I'll need to have a kidney transplant. I wondered if you would consider being a donor."

Now I was becoming overwhelmed. I told her about Greg being gone and all and I just needed some time to think. I felt badly later, thinking that I should have just uttered, "Why, sure."

Finally, he called. I asked him how the weather was in Florida, but he didn't answer.

"Greg, I've had something come up in the family and I'm wondering when you're coming home?"

"Like what?"

"My sister, Terry's not well. Her doctor said she needs a kidney transplant and wants me to consider being a donor."

"Hey, if you go ahead and agree to do something stupid like that, I'll divorce you."

"What? How can you mean that? What if it was one of your brothers? You mean that you wouldn't do it for one of them?"

"Nope. That's why the strong survive. See ya." The line went dead.

I hung up the phone and wondered what had happened to the man that I married. What had made him so cold and unfeeling?

A few days later, things became stranger. He called with a bizarre request.

"Hi. I'm driving home. Don't tell anyone that I'm coming. Have the garage door open for me. See you in a little while."

I became alarmed. Why was he being so secretive? What was all the mystery? I phoned a friend of mine so someone would know what he said – in case something happened.

He pulled in the driveway shortly afterward with his headlights off, parked in the garage and immediately put the door down. He looked rested and he was affectionate; we made love that night.

"I'm heading up north tomorrow morning to meet with the accountant. I'll be back in a few days." He didn't talk about his trip, the business or anything. It was very quiet in the house.

The appointment had been made for Terry and the family members to meet at Beaumont Hospital for the testing regarding the kidney transplant. Each one of us had our blood drawn and met with a psychologist who asked each of us some questions. She asked me if there was any reason I would have any hesitation being a donor. I wanted to tell her what was troubling me.

"My husband told me that if I agreed to donate a kidney, he'd divorce me."

She looked surprised. "How did that make you feel?"

"Like I don't know who he is anymore, but I won't let a remark like that stop me."

She got me a tissue to blot my eyes. I said goodbye to my family, left the hospital and headed back to beauty college.

Within the year, my sister, Terry got her transplant. I was only a twenty-five percent match; I didn't make the grade. Mom was closer, but the doctor wanted a higher percentage match. My sister Robin hadn't been tested because she and her husband were trying to get pregnant. After several months, Robin decided to get tested anyway and was a one-hundred percent match. Robin was willing and the transplant took place, saving Terry the angst of kidney dialysis. That's what people who love each other do.

Chapter 39

I LOVE YOU, GOODBYE

Greg returned home in a couple of days from up north and there appeared to be a return to normalcy. In the meantime, I had gotten my real estate license renewal in the mail. Greg had complained about me paying my real estate dues which I kept up with since we'd gotten married.

"Why do you want to pay on something you'll never need to use again? We've got a great business going and that's going to expand. There's no need to think about selling real estate anymore." So, I let the due date pass by and threw my license renewal in the waste basket.

It was in May of 1993, the trees had begun to blossom and we were able to get away with wearing warm sweaters while the sun was out. He called me from the club in the afternoon.

"Hi, I'll be home in a couple of hours. Would you like to grab a bite to eat with me? Are you getting hungry?"

"Yes I am hungry, but I can wait for you. I'll just fix a piece of toast and applesauce."

He almost sounded cheerful and I was relieved he seemed more like himself. A few hours later, he pulled in the driveway and beeped the horn twice. I came out and got into the car.

"So, what have you been doing today?" I asked innocently.

"What the hell do you think I've been doing? Why are you questioning me? It's none of your f___ing business what I've been doing."

I said, "Stop the car . . . I'm getting out." I reached for the door handle as he grabbed my left arm firmly and started squeezing hard at the bicep while pulling me back into the car.

"You're not going anywhere except with me, you got it?"

He started driving down Elizabeth Lake Road at a high rate of speed. We ended up at one of my favorite restaurants, The Lazy Lion in Keego Harbor.

"Let's go, Babycakes," he snarled.

I was afraid to go in. I thought he'd make a scene. Instead, a man that we had both gone to school with seated us. He had been on the football team and the track team in high school and was a great athlete. I had always wondered if he went on to bigger things in college.

"So, what have you been up to?" Greg asked him.

"I'm a manager here, not much else."

We looked at the menu. I had lost my appetite and felt sick to my stomach.

Greg ordered and the waitress glanced at me and waited.

"I'm not really hungry right now. Just bring me some tea."

Greg grabbed my leg under the table and began to grip it tightly. "Order something!" he demanded.

"Okay, bring me a grilled chicken salad," I said without looking up, as tears welled up in my eyes.

He began to eat while I methodically played "move the salad" in the bowl. He glanced over at the manager and then said to me, "You know what? I hit him during a football scrimmage so hard that it put him out of commission. I don't think he was even able to run track after that," he gloated.

It made me feel sicker. I looked over at this promising athlete and sadly had to turn away. What had he done to Greg that he ever deserved to get roughed up that way? What had I done?

I thought we'd never leave the restaurant. The waitress boxed up my salad and our old high schoolmate rang up our bill saying, "It's been good seeing you."

When we got home, Greg fell asleep on the sofa and I was glad. No more chance for confrontation, I thought. The following day, I bought some trays of flowers to put around the perimeter of the house. I was outdoors most of the day, while Greg was in and out.

"I've got to grab a shower before I head to the club. I have to cover the game room tonight," he announced as he headed indoors. Later, I was putting the gardening tools away when he joined me in the garage. He was wearing one of his dark turquoise Spanky's sport shirts that we had specially made for all the guys to wear when they were working. The scent of his cologne was in the air. He embraced me, then picked me right up off the floor and twirled me around.

I began to laugh and said, "Greg, put me down . . . I'm going to get you all dirty." My hands and arms were speckled with black dirt.

As he set me back down, he kissed me and said, "I love you . . . goodbye," and then he was gone. I chuckled to myself and smiled, wondering what had gotten into him. About half an hour later, I headed into the house for a warm shower. As I reached into the linen closet for a clean towel, something just didn't look right. His toiletries were gone. There was no deodorant, no toothbrush, and no cologne in sight. Apprehensive, I checked his closet. Empty hangers filled his side and his suitcase was missing. I nervously splashed off in the shower, quickly dressed, and headed for the club. Mark was at the door when I got there. I wanted an explanation.

"You can't come in—Greg's orders," Mark said nervously.

I was seething. "You get the hell out of my way, Mark. I want to talk to him now!"

As I pushed by him, he spouted, "He's not here . . . he's at his girlfriend's."

I stopped in my tracks. So, that's what it was all about. Greg had left me. I was stunned and shaking. I got back into my car and drove over to my parents' house. Mom stood holding a dish towel as I blurted out what had occurred in less than a minute. I was beside myself, angry and frustrated pacing back and forth across their front lawn. She stayed in the house, powerless to offer me any comfort. There was no one I could call and vent to that would understand what I was feeling. I was stuck inside this human volcano.

I sat up that night in the living room dissecting what had happened. Obviously, my efforts at being the understanding wife had been futile. I couldn't sleep. I rummaged through the garbage bag looking for my real estate license renewal form. The bag I'd dropped it in was already gone. I'd have to call the State of Michigan real estate licensing division in Lansing tomorrow, I thought. Maybe it's not too late. It was after three in the morning when I heard the front door open. Greg sauntered in carrying his suitcase.

"What did she do, throw you out?" I glared at him and punctuated my words.

"No, she wants to live here."

"Well, there is no way she is moving into this house."

"Oh, yes she will, because you will be leaving – one way or the other. Oh, and by the way, she wants her earrings back."

Chapter 40

STANDING GROUND, LYING DOWN, NEARLY DROWN

It didn't take long before things turned from bad to worse. Greg insisted on staying at the house while he considered how he wanted to end our marriage. His mood swings were horrendous and volatile. My emotional state was running on fumes. I had been pushed right out of a business that had been "ours" in my eyes. I was listed at secretary-treasurer of Sundown Disco on the paperwork when we bought Tom out of the business. My name was on every loan and my car was used as collateral on our building lease. I was right in the middle of a year of beauty college, all for the sake of expanding our business. I was not going to be pushed out of my home now, too. Greg began staying in the guest room with his drum set. I stayed in the master bedroom and had a single cylinder deadbolt lock installed on the door. The new routine was that I'd leave for beauty college in the morning while Greg slept, and he would leave for the club late in the afternoon. I'd return home from school and later head to bed in my room, and he'd come in at three or four in the morning and go to bed in his room. The only hint of two people living in the house was the steam on the bathroom mirror from a shower he'd take in the afternoon before leaving for parts unknown.

There was no restful sleeping in the house. I'd hear him wandering around; sometimes he'd even start playing his drums in the wee hours which had the neighbors griping at me in the driveway the following days. On the night after I had the lock installed on the bedroom door, he came home at three-thirty a.m., marched to my room and tried but couldn't get in. Then the screaming began as he fought with the doorknob.

"Open this Goddamn door, do you hear me?"

"Leave me alone, Greg, and go to bed."

'I want to talk to you . . . open this door or I'll break it down! You better talk to me if you know what's good for you."

He began kicking the door rapaciously. A dark fear came over me. He was acting like a crazed maniac. Then it suddenly stopped. I heard his footsteps as he trudged away from the door.

"Please come and talk to me, just talk to me . . ." he said in a quiet voice from the living room.

He sounded different, pathetic and subdued. I opened the door slowly with my bathrobe wrapped tightly around me. Upon entering the living room, he was lying naked on the massive sofa, curled up in the fetal position.

"I just couldn't do it without you and now here we are," he said in a whimpering voice.

"What's so bad about that, Greg? Why do you have such a problem with that? I loved you and that's what people that love each other do. What was wrong with me helping you?"

"Everything."

It was senseless trying to talk to him. I returned to my room and relocked the door. It was eerily quiet as I tried to sleep for a few hours.

I began to lose weight. In the next three weeks I would lose eighteen pounds. I barely had an appetite and when I did, the stress seemed to burn the calories away. I had stopped buying groceries. When I checked our bank account after finding out he had a mistress, I discovered he'd removed all of the money except for five hundred dollars. I removed two hundred fifty dollars until I could talk to a lawyer about the rest. My lawyer friend was hesitant to take me as a client because of the work his firm had done with our business when we had bought out Greg's partner. David was concerned it may be a conflict of interest.

Returning home after school a few days later, I changed out of my white uniform, into a red sweatshirt and a pair of jeans, and foraged for something to eat in the refrigerator. There was nearly a full jar of applesauce and a partial loaf of bread, so I had my old standby; toast covered in applesauce.

It wasn't long after that I doubled over in pain with nausea, shaky and sweating. I fell onto the bedroom floor, but had no strength to get back up, so I began slowly crawling down the hallway to the bathroom. I was going to be sick. I threw up a few times and began shaking violently as if I was having a seizure and then passed out on the cold tile floor in my own vomit. When I awoke, I was very cold and the bathroom was dark. I was having trouble with my arms and legs. They felt numb and heavy. All I wanted to do was feel better. I'd found when I was younger and had cramps, the flu, or bronchitis, what made me more comfortable was being immersed under water up to my neck, the hotter the better and I would try to sweat it out. So, I tried reaching over the edge of the bathtub, attempting to close the drain and turn on the water faucets. My arms just wouldn't work. It took several attempts and seemed like an insurmountable task, but somehow I managed to fill the tub, and then threw myself over the tub edge fully dressed. I used my feet to turn off the water before I collapsed now immersed in the water, exhausted and shivering.

The house seemed to have taken on the chill. I had never felt so sick and vulnerable. I was scared I was going to die. A few times, I awoke as my head slid down in the tub and I began inhaling water through my nose causing me to choke. I was swallowing a lot of water. Panicked, I'd try to push with my feet to get my nose above water level and would barely move an inch. Strangely enough, something incredible happened. My body totally relaxed and an unbelievable calm came over me. I was at peace for awhile.

It seemed as though I'd been lying there for hours. The water encircling me was cold. The bathroom door opened and the light came on. As I slowly opened my eyes, I saw this look of disbelief on Greg's face.

He stared at me, then would look away and then stare again, looking perplexed. I wondered if he was aggravated that I was still alive. Finally he spoke to me.

"You want some help?" he growled, not moving a muscle toward me while he stood steadfastly in the doorway.

"Why is it so cold in the house?" I mumbled to him as my teeth chattered.

"Because I turned the heat off, that's why. I wasn't gonna waste another dime on you here."

I just wanted him to stay away from me. All he had to do is walk over and push my head under the water and I knew I would drown. I couldn't protect myself – I couldn't even lift my fingers. As quietly as he came in, he turned and then stormed out of the bathroom, turning off the light to leave me lying there once again in the dark, slamming the bathroom door on his way out. I was alone again.

The next day a little after eleven a.m., I had the strength to crawl out of the bathtub. I'd been under the water for about eighteen hours. I swear there must have been an angel with me. Maybe that was why the calm had swept over me. I clawed at my wet clothes until they were off, and wrapped up in a terry cloth robe. I stumbled into the kitchen and opened the door leading into the garage. It was such a relief that Greg's car was gone. On a hunch, I peered into the refrigerator. The jar of applesauce was missing. Then I limped down the stairs into the basement to check and see if the boiler was shut down. There still was no heat in the house. While down there, a peculiar thought crossed my mind and I scanned a shelf in the unfinished part of the basement. There had been a box of rat poison left there by the previous owners. It was missing, too. My remaining days in the house, I ate nothing that I didn't bring home with me.

Chapter 41

A NINE MILLIMETER RULES

It would take a few days before Greg began looking for his gun. I had hidden it because his irrational behavior had become much more frequent and severe. I came home from school and found he had rifled through my belongings and dumped drawers of clothes on the floor. The gun was now in his shoulder holster slung over the headboard in my room with the barrel pointed into my pillow. It was my warning. My brother, Brad had come over, took one look and told me he would be back to stay at the house with me. I let Greg know when he stopped by the house.

"No one else is going to be living in this house – have you got that?"

Just then, Brad knocked on the door. He and I left the house to get something to eat. I told him what Greg had said, but it didn't faze Brad – it just made him angry. I was afraid someone was going to get hurt, and I feared for myself, too. When we returned to the house, Greg had left. Brad stayed with me until quite late. I locked myself in my bedroom and tried to sleep but couldn't.

The next day at beauty college, the pressure of all of it had gotten to me and I cracked. I began sobbing and left out the back door of the building. Greg had threatened to have the divorce papers served on me there, so each day became a waiting game. He also insisted I move out and back into my original home which our manager was renting. Mark had not moved so I couldn't move.

It was early morning, 4:15 a.m. on June 21st when all hell broke loose. Greg came home on a rampage, forced my bedroom door open, screaming, "Bitch, you bitch! I want you outta here, now!" while he waved his gun in my face. I grabbed some clothes, threw on a bathrobe, got the car keys and ran out of the house. That was the last night I stayed on Motorway Drive.

The following day, my brother-in-law, Larry returned to the house with me after the Waterford Police gave the go ahead for him to be my police presence. I had called Greg and said "I need to come over so I can get my clothes." He was surprised when he opened the door and saw Larry. He seemed to understand now was not the time to get lippy.

"Go get your guns, Greg, all of them and bring them out here."

He disappeared back into the house and returned with a long gun and his nine millimeter. I had told Larry that I knew of two long guns and his hand gun.

"Where's the other one, Greg?"

"That's all there is—that's it."

"It better be, Greg, because if she comes in and you do anything to hurt her, I will blow your head off."

Greg followed me into the bedroom while I quickly gathered up an armful of clothing from the closet and drawers.

"So you had to bring the big guns with you, eh?"

I didn't answer him . . . just kept moving. I tossed a few pairs of shoes in a box with several of my books, one of which was my 1968 high school yearbook. Life was so much simpler then. Within five minutes, I was back out the front door and in the car. I'd stay at my parents for the time being.

On June 25, 1983 and ten days before my thirty-third birthday, I was able to move back into my small home I had built on Morningside Drive, less than a quarter mile from the Motorway house. Each time I drove by Greg's and my house, I couldn't help but glance over at the bathroom window which faced Cooley Lake Road. The infamous bathtub incident just sickened me and made me realize how close I came to losing my life that night, how stupid it made me feel, and how humiliating the entire ordeal was. Two of my brother-in-laws, Walt and Larry stayed by me during the move. They were a godsend.

My piano was slightly damaged in the move which was a small price to pay compared to what could have been.

Chapter 42

LAWYERS:
Spread Sheets
Buy a Gun and Make a Will
Lipstick

My quest in finding an attorney started in early June. On the advice of the beauty college manager, a savvy lady named Judy, I hired an attorney named James out of Southfield, Michigan. My first visit to him was on June 9, 1983 and a retainer was paid that day. An incident happened the evening of June 9th and I was upset when I contacted him the next day. He was cold and sarcastic on the phone. I fired him.

The next attorney was recommended by a judge that my parents knew. I met with Rick on June 10th and hired him. I wasn't optimistic about the choice, but felt surely if a judge was going to say he'd want his own daughter to hire this man for divorce purposes, I should heed his advice. As I was thumbing through my books which were in a box along with clothing and the shoes I'd grabbed while in the house, I discovered a very interesting document. Tucked inside my class yearbook was a series of spreadsheets detailing the name and value of each video game, and figures, such as "4K," "8K" along with other information. I didn't know at the time exactly what I had. Greg and I both had the same yearbook sitting in the bookcase, each one signed by our own school chums. I surmised that he must have thought he put the papers in his book and not mine. When I took the sheets with me to show my attorney on our next visit, his reaction was more than merely surprise.

"Where did you say you found these? Geez, Beth, do you know what these are? You can't leave these here in my office. Somebody may want to burn this place down for them. Get them out of here, and hide them in a safe place. And for your sake, buy a gun and make a will."

I was shaken when I left his office. I told my parents what Rick had said and they looked worried. We decided the documents would be hidden in a heating duct. I couldn't afford a gun and asked Dad if I could borrow one. At first he agreed, but after some thought, he declined. I had been so stressed; he may have thought I'd use it on myself. I did have a will drawn up and on file within the year.

In the coming weeks, I was bounced back and forth between two attorneys at this firm, Rick to Tom, and Tom back to Rick. I never knew who would be representing me in court until the night before. I was missing this connection I wanted to have with my lawyer. I had only been living back in my home on Morningside for a few days. There had always been a double cylinder deadbolt lock and a thumb turn lock on the back door. I wanted the locks changed, but could only afford to change one, so my father helped me replace the thumb turn lock. I barely slept at night, just dosing at times. The stress began to cause my hair to fall out.

At least with a different lock on the door, maybe I would feel more secure. Then, about two-thirty in the morning, I heard someone at the back door trying to get in. In anger, I jumped out of bed in the dark and ran at the back door, slamming my body full force into it.

"Get away from here . . . I'm calling the police!" I screamed at the top of my lungs, and pounded my fists on the door. I slid down onto the kitchen floor and sobbed. I just wanted to be left alone. Minutes went by before I got up and slowly peered outdoors. There gleaming in the doorknob was a set of keys that would have worked a day earlier. It was my good fortune they didn't have the latest key. If I had gotten a gun, I know I would have fired through the door. I began sleeping with a large knife under my pillow.

I had an appointment with Tom, the attorney the next morning. When I arrived and was seated in his office, I tearfully told him about the previous evening's events and my visitor with a set of keys. I was very distraught, and as I looked across the desk at him, he began to chuckle.

"What do you think is so funny?" I asked, pissed that I had to deal with him.

"Oh, uh, you've got lipstick on your tooth," as he pointed to his own front tooth and grinned.

"You know, if this is the best you can do, I don't know that I want you representing me. I'm having a rough time here in case you haven't noticed."

I will never forget that moment, a laughable one for him, that is. Hiring a lawyer can be such a joke, especially when they show such a lack of professionalism. But, I did go through with a meeting scheduled by Greg's attorney that day accompanied by Mister Funny Man. Greg waited in the lobby which was a good thing. I wanted to rip him in half for having someone try to break in my home and most likely, with his keys.

Chapter 43

BEAUTY SCHOOL SANITY AND LAUGHTER WHILE UNDERCOVERS WONDER

In the fall of 1993, court or lawyer's appointments seemed to have become a large part of my life. I had barely crossed the halfway point through beauty college at the time divorce proceedings had begun, but I still felt my decision to stick with it and finish was emotionally and mentally a good one. I know I would have lost my mind if it hadn't been for the incredible friendships and camaraderie I found there. Even with the strong smells of perm solution, hairsprays, nail polish and polish removers constantly in the air, it seemed like home to me. So many times, I felt like I was crying on the inside, but there was always another student that would provide a belly laugh for all of us. I have yet to laugh so much in one year as I did there, in spite of the circumstances.

There were at least fifteen of us enrolled together and four were men. I have one picture of us, all dressed in white looking the part. Out of site were the mannequin heads that we used to perfect our wave, roller, and perm rod techniques. Then there was the eclectic side of our group. Dianna was the resident psychic. Sometimes she'd do tarot card readings in the break room on our lunch hours. Sharon had a sister working at a swanky salon in Birmingham and had aspirations of working there. Teresa was laid off from one of the automotive plants. Kip's mother had recently died and he was trying to focus on a new vocation. Susie was going through a very tough divorce involving abuse of her kids. Everybody had a story to tell.

During the first week of school in January of 1993, I realized that there was no refrigerator in the break room and I planned on bringing my lunch daily. Greg and I had an unused refrigerator that was left in the house we bought, so we donated to the school. He and Mark brought it over and set it up in the break room. That was to be the last kindness shown to me.

Who knew that six months later I would be moving back to my house on Morningside? Things had grown increasingly tense. I couldn't sleep after the near break-in, which left me nervous and edgy. Now, about a third of my hair had fallen out along with most of my eyelashes. At night, a visitor would crouch down outside of my bedroom window smoking cigarettes and trampling my day lilies. The smoke would waft in as I struggled to fall asleep. Calls to the police were fruitless. Some nights, my parents would drive by, and then Mom would call me immediately about seeing "someone out there." I was told by the police that unless I had an unwanted intruder entering my home, there was no crime, not even trespassing.

One night, I got a knock on the front door. I looked out the blinds, fearful of anyone hanging around. It was a couple of guys, one with a familiar face that belonged to a fellow who worked at Spanky's for awhile, and then left the state with his girlfriend. Before they left town, the couple came to see me with flowers and told me how sorry they were to hear about what had happened between Greg and me. It had only been about four months since they'd left. What brought him to my house, I wondered as I cautiously opened the door.

"Greg owes me some money, quite a bit of money and I came for it."

"I didn't know you were back in town. Why would you come to me for money he owes you? If you think there's some stashed here, you're mistaken. I'm barely getting by myself. What does he owe you money for?"

"Some drugs."

"What kind of drugs?

"Cocaine."

"Oh, and you think you coming over here would do what? You take it up with him, the slime, and don't come back here again." I shuddered after slamming the door.

I hadn't known Greg was using cocaine; in fact I'd never been close to anyone that did. It seemed so stupidly naïve to me now. But it all seemed to fall into place—the severe mood swings, weight loss, black circles around his eyes, paranoia, threatening behavior, playing drums for hours and hours in a row. I would have never done drugs with him and he knew that. We shared an occasional marijuana cigarette which I'm not proud of, but that was the extent of it. Maybe his girlfriend was more willing to do the hard drugs with him.

I had lunch over at Mom's one afternoon and she had something on her mind. I knew "the look."

"Your dad and I talked it over and wondered if you'd want to get out of Michigan and go down to Florida for awhile. You can stay at our condo. It seems harder everyday to see what this is doing to you here. We worry about you. Will you go?"

"Mom, I know I'd feel safer, but I'm still in school. I'd like to finish something I've started. I have no real estate license anymore. Let me talk to my attorney about it."

The more I thought it over, the more I wanted to leave town. I called Rick and had a brief conversation about it.

But it was not to be. A few days later, Rick called and gave me some disheartening news.

"I mentioned about you possibly leaving town to Greg's attorney. He told Greg about it and Greg fired back that if you leave, he will find a way to drag you back here each and every week until this divorce is settled. It could get costly for you flying back and forth. I don't know if it would be worth it, Beth."

"I'm sorry . . . exactly what IS the price tag for sanity?" I retorted. It seemed defeating.

One day shortly after, I received what seemed like a breath of fresh air. Steve, my former real estate broker and I ran into one another. He had been through a recent divorce and was now living in an apartment. I told him about my mess that was in the making. His eyes showed me what I needed; that he cared. We both signed up for a local photography class nearby. He gave me a crash course in motorcycles and took me to a college parking lot to practice. He taught me to ride and then loaned me one of his bikes to use. It was nice being distracted from the legal madness.

"You know, Steve, it was in May that my real estate license had come due for renewal. When I began to fill out the paperwork, Greg gave me this big speech about us having this solid business and that I'd never have to resort to selling real estate again. Within three weeks, he had left me and the chaos began. I dug through all the trash for my renewal papers and they were already in a garbage truck somewhere. I called the State and they told me I was too late, that I'd have to take the real estate courses all over again along with the State exam. I was caught with no other way to make a living except for the working at our club and now I can't even do that. I've really made some poor choices in my life. Being with Greg has turned out to be the worst mistake I've ever made and giving up my real estate license was really foolish."

My attorney had advised me not to be seen out with any men while the divorce was in process, even though it seemed fine for Greg to be with his girlfriend. I had a hard time accepting that, knowing she was living in my house, sleeping in bed every night with my husband and it made no difference at all. Steve and I stayed in mostly, at his place or mine. He helped me rake my leaves, clean my gutters, and even loaned me his service uniform to wear to the beauty college on Halloween. We were comfortable with each other.

The outdoor windows on the house hadn't been washed since I moved back in, so I gathered together my supplies and got started. When I worked my way around to the back kitchen window, there was a surprise waiting for me. Strands of monofilament line were stretched across the window casing in the shape of a cross, with a very small silver disk anchored in the center. I carefully and curiously took it down and then called an old police friend named Dallas, who had gone into private investigation after he retired. I had done a few small investigative jobs with him. He said to stop over and he'd look at what I found. I thought it was a bug.

"Listen Beth, I'd like to send it off to a buddy of mine with the State Police. I'll let you know when I hear something."

It was about a week later when Dallas called. I was anxious to find out what it was, why it was there, and anything that would make sense.

"Got you some information, Beth and you won't like it. They said it was one of the best bugs they've seen. Now, who and why would anybody feel the need to bug your house?"

I told him about the papers I'd run across and what my attorney had said. Dallas looked at me and said, "I agree with him. You should have a gun . . . this changes things."

Fall was fleeting. Beauty college was going to be finished in a few months and I had no idea if I would be able to make a decent living as a cosmetologist. In the meantime, Steve had moved into a house he owned where he had let renters stay at times. It was a brisk, but sunny Sunday afternoon and Steve and I were being lazy watching an NFL football game on television. Steve was lying on the sofa with his head in my lap when he dozed off during halftime. The sunshine streaming in the windows made the room feel warm and cozy. Then I heard him gasp while his arms suddenly raised and he grabbed my throat with both hands. He was ranting in a language I didn't recognize. I tugged at his hands while trying to yell to him, "Steve, Steve, it's me … Beth." When I was able to wake him, he had a startled look on his face.

"What happened? Was I dreaming? What's wrong?"

"You were choking me, and talking in a foreign language. You really scared me," I mumbled as I rubbed my throat and then I told him what he had been calling out.

"It was Vietnamese," he said softly, looking shaken and turning away. After being out of the military for eighteen years, it was his first flashback from the Viet Nam War, very unsettling for him and for me. He began drinking more and we gradually drifted apart with him telling me one day, "I can't give you what you need."

A few weeks passed when I was pulled over by the Michigan State Police on Telegraph Road and was asked to follow them to the Police Post.

"Why? What did I do? I wasn't speeding."

"We were asked to bring you in to answer some questions."

"Who asked you? Questions about what?"

"Everything will be explained to you when we get there."

I was taken into a small room with a few chairs. Within five minutes, a husky, young man walked in wearing jeans and a tee shirt and no I.D. badge. I asked to see his identification; he was with the Narcotic Enforcement Team. I wondered then whether there was connection between my conversation with Dallas and me ending up here.

"We've been doing an investigation, and it seems that some people of interest have been seen frequently at your house."

"Listen, I've been going through a nasty divorce and I'd like to let my attorney know about this. Could I please call him?

"Sure, I'll wait."

I nervously called Rick, who simply said, "Just cooperate with them, Beth. Tell them what they want to know."

"Will you be coming down here, Rick?"

"No, you don't need me there," he said and then hung up.

I'd never been questioned before by the police. In fact, I'd never even gotten a ticket, so it was unnerving. I wanted to get this straightened out, but first I needed to know which house he was talking about.

"So, was this at the house on Motorway or the house on Morningside?"

"Well, the house on Motorway, where you live."

"Sir, I haven't lived there in over four months. In fact, I left at gunpoint in the middle of the night and went back one time with a policeman to get my clothes. My husband lives there with his girlfriend, not me. I have no idea who's been at the house with them." Some pretty lousy surveillance, I thought.

"Maybe a few of these names will be familiar. Take a look," he said, pushing a notepad over in front of me. The name on top was our video game distributor, whose company held the paper on the ninety-three thousand dollar loan – the same person who had the private meetings with Greg out of earshot. The green spreadsheets I had tucked away were about their dealings.

"Yeah, I know this person. He came over a few times, but Greg talked to him more on the phone and didn't discuss much of any business in front of me. They'd take off for lunch together or walk down to the lake."

There were more questions about the man and if we'd spent time at his home or with anyone else in his family. Greg and I had gone to their home once or twice. There wasn't much more that interested the policeman. Then he let me go home, only to contemplate what surprises would be next.

Chapter 44

DESPAIR REIGNS

In late December, I was finished with beauty college. It was hustle and bustle as my fellow students one by one left for parts unknown. We were each on a mission to carve out a living for ourselves and be happy. I kept myself busy writing my resumé with a plan to try and get into one of the cosmetics companies. I felt I should have a picture on my resumé, so I called a local photographer, also named Beth, and made an appointment for a sitting. When I arrived a few days later for my appointment, we talked about my financial situation.

"I'll have to have my pictures taken in black and white. I just can't afford color photos."

"Oh come on, we need to shoot them in color. Are you sure? I'll work out a payment arrangement for you."

"No, I can't. I just don't need any debt right now."

The photographer rolled her eyes a bit and said, "Well, okay . . . let's get started."

It was a simple, yet elegant look. I wore a silky, cream colored blouse with a mandarin collar. My freshly painted deep wine colored fingernails and gold earrings, along with a gold initial ring Ray had given me one year capped off the look. I was anxious to get the prints back and start looking for work. It was going to take a few weeks to get my resumé distributed.

Time dragged on with more divorce issues. A local bank sent me papers regarding a twenty thousand dollar ninety day note that was now in arrears. The main problem was that I had never signed for the loan. I was furious that forgery had now taken place. After a talk with my folks, I had the name of the president of the bank and made an "urgent" appointment to see him, mentioning that I was Naomi's daughter. Greg had become quite good friends with one of the bank vice presidents and I felt that the two were connected. Maybe they were even doing coke together. My appointment with the bank president couldn't come soon enough.

"Thanks for seeing me. First of all, I never took out this loan with your bank. Secondly, this is not my signature. It's a forgery.

Third, you better take a long and hard look at this man in your bank that has gotten so chummy with my husband. Oh, and a drug test might be in order."

"Well, we certainly would be willing to work out some type of payment program . . . "

"Listen to me, you need to investigate this! I am not responsible for this. If you do not believe me, get a handwriting expert in here! If I am contacted again about this forgery, I will go to every newspaper and television station that will listen to me and tell them how your bank let this man put one over on you . . . and you need to check out your employee!"

I was proud of myself for standing my ground. Back in November of 1983, I had to meet with the certified public accountants firm handling the audit of Spanky's. Then in December there were orders for depositions. In January of 1984 came the default of the promissory note to the distributing company for over fifty-nine thousand dollars, with more depositions to give, subpoenas to be received, and I was still owed money in back alimony; Greg had stopped paying on January 16, 1984. I received confirmation of my date to take the Cosmetology State Boards; it was February 15th. I had to borrow five hundred dollars to pay my house payment and health insurance. On February 21st, I was required to send a letter to the assigned judge.

In the meantime, I drove by the Motorway house and saw a for sale sign in the yard. No one had contacted me from the real estate office letting me know my house was listed. I thought it was a strange way to do business, but what also concerned me were the latent defects in the home that I did not want to turn into a lawsuit. Sewage backups and non-working heat in parts of the house were major issues. I rode into Clarkston with my father who was going to visit Grandma Griffin. He dropped me off at the main corner downtown and continued on his way. I began to walk to the real estate office involved. On my way, I was muttering to myself as I cut through Rudy's Market parking lot. A stake truck was backing up and hit me, knocking me to the pavement. The driver must have felt the thump because he stopped short of driving over my legs. My knees were bleeding as the driver jumped out of his truck and ran around to the back.

"Oh, my God, are you hurt? God, I'm so sorry. What can I do?"

"Nothing. I'll be alright. No harm done on purpose—I know that."

He helped me up off the ground, and I brushed my clothes off. I was fired up as I headed toward the office. Once there, I very definitively explained who I was and why I was there and my dismay at finding out by a real estate sign that my house on Motorway was listed.

"I need to borrow a typewriter. I'm not leaving here until I give you a list of known defects I'm aware of. What you do with it is up to you, but I want to be held harmless. You'll need to sign and date this and I want it notarized."

I began to type furiously while the broker stood reading over my shoulder. When I was finished with the letter complete with lines for signatures, dates, and notary space, she spoke up.

"Let say this . . . if you ever decide to sell real estate again, I'd appreciate it if you would come and work for me. I'd like you on my team, okay?"

I began to walk in the direction of my aunt and uncle's house where Grandma was living. My knees had stopped bleeding, but the wounds had begun to sting and my left hip felt numb and was starting to swell. So, I sat on a park bench and watched for Dad's car, flagging him down.

"What happened to you?" he questioned glancing down at my knees.

"I just got hit by a truck in Rudy's Market parking lot. I think it scared the driver worse than it scared me. I'm okay. Let's go."

Then it was back to court over the temporary alimony issue. Also, there was legal notice of more depositions coming up the end of the month. I began to close myself off from the world, rarely leaving my house. I preferred my blinds closed and most lights off. My depression was consuming.

Mom came by and knocked several times before I let her in. She was irritated at first until she got a good look at me. I was a mess.

"What's happening to you? Aren't you sleeping? What's got you looking so sad?"

I didn't turn to look at her. I just stared at the floor.

"I have no peace in my life, Mom, no peace and I don't know if I can hang on until I do."

"What can I do for you, honey? Why don't you come and stay with Dad and me for awhile?"

"No, you don't need that—nobody does."

She left to go make dinner for her and my dad while I made a plan. I drove to the drug store two miles away and bought a gallon of vodka. Then I rummaged through the medicine cabinet and the linen closet while feeling incredibly exhausted. I needed to get a few things in order first. I would take my life the following day.

Chapter 45

WANNA BE A MODEL FOR A DAY?

It was about eleven the next day when I methodically lined up all the pill bottles I could find on the dining room table. I had a tall glass in front of me, wondering whether to put ice in the glass to make the vodka go down easier. I'd never been a huge fan of vodka, but I knew that the amount of scotch it could take would probably make me throw up and ruin everything. I poured the vodka nearly to the brim, and was just about to down my first gulp with the first handful of pills when the phone rang. I let it ring five or six times but whoever it was wasn't giving up. It was aggravating. Begrudgingly I said hello. It was the photographer.

"Listen Beth, I've had this idea of photographing someone posing as a forties or fifties movie actress for a competition I'd like to enter. I'd really like for you to be my model. You were really easy to work with when I took your resumé pictures and you look the part. Would you do it?"

What timing, I thought. Just give me a reason to say no.

"When would that be?" I asked as I fiddled taking the lids off more pill bottles.

"Day after tomorrow, about eleven o'clock would be great . . . hello? Are you there?"

"Oh . . . yeah, I was thinking it over. After hesitating again, I said "Okay, I'll do it" with no enthusiasm whatsoever. Maybe she'll be put off about my lack of eagerness and call the whole thing off, I thought hanging up.

Then someone began knocking on my front door. It could be a family member since two of my sisters, one brother and my parents lived in the neighborhood. Quickly gathering up the pill bottles and the vodka, I stuffed them all in the refrigerator. It turned out to be a neighbor with some political petition. I wasn't amused, but at least I was feeling something other than depression. I signed the petition and then a question occurred to me. Does your signature count if you die after you've signed it? It's strange what you think about.

I made a quick call to the photographer the next day to find out what I should bring with me to the sitting.

"Just bring several pairs of earrings and your makeup bag. I'll probably have something here that I'll want you to wear."

I was set. The following day, I was sitting in the photographer's studio on Dixie Highway. She positioned me in several poses but wasn't really obtaining the results she wanted.

"Hmmmm . . . I'm just not seeing what I was looking for. Let's try you in this rattan chair. Now, how about wearing this?"

It was a turban-shaped headdress with veiling attached. She had me turn partially toward the camera then away. I sat motionless while she made camera adjustments. I had done my own makeup and had put on a delicate pair of small pearl and silver earrings. I was actually enjoying myself which was long overdue. She told me it would take several days of special processing before she'd have the proofs and decide if the results met her expectations.

A few days later, the phone rang as I sat back in my cocoon of a house. It was the photographer.

"Beth, I'm so excited! Meteor Photo just called and they said we've got a winner! One of our pictures blew them away. That will be my entry in the competition. Thank you so much for working with me on this."

I was happy for her. She sounded exuberant on the phone. The blue ribbon photo was selected for exhibition in state and regional competitions and there was a possibility it would later go on display to tour the world. We spoke on the phone after she received the judging comments. Apparently, several of the judges came up with the same conclusion regarding my picture. The photo which she entitled, "Sheer Sophistication" was considered to have an "eerie quality" mentioned by several of them. I instantly knew what it was. When I saw the picture I felt as if I were looking into my own soul through the eyes looking back at me. I had been on the brink of suicide. It was all there; I saw myself as transparent. Months later, I drove by the studio and saw the photo enlarged many times up in lights on the business marquee, those same eyes looking back at me, haunting me.

I decided to write a thank you note to the photographer. In it, I explained to her that at the moment she called and ask me to pose for her, my plan to terminate my life was in progress. That phone call in essence saved my life and gave me some hope. Contrary to Greg's comments to me that "you're worthless and no one will ever want you," I felt that maybe I was worthwhile after all.

Chapter 46

RESUMÉ FOR JACQUELINE OF ALL TRADES

My cosmetology resumé was getting very few bites, and literally none in the cosmetic field. A few beauty salons were willing to hire me as a "shampoo girl" but I knew the earning potential would be too limited to sustain me. If my work had been as a second income, I would have stuck with it until I could get my own chair. I just didn't have time to wait for success.

After pouring over the want ads in several papers, I spotted something of interest. Dean Witter Reynolds was hiring for a new office to be opened in Southfield. It was an opportunity to interview and test for a position to train as a stockbroker with their firm. I went to the interview, took the entrance exam which had questions involving calculus. I'd always struggled with math and missed the cut by two points. However, they would need sales assistants for the brokers and I was willing to start there. Once working under their roof I was told that it would be possible to be sponsored by Dean Witter Reynolds and study for the Series 7 exam to become a broker that way. I was game. I knew Granddad would be proud of me if I made it that far. My first exposure to the stock market was when I went to visit him and Grandma in Boynton Beach, Florida during spring break my senior year of high school. Their condo was on the Intercostals, and only about a mile from the ocean. I wanted to spend lazy afternoons flirting with guys at the beach; he insisted we make a daily afternoon trip to the stock market in West Palm Beach. He'd sit and smoke a cigar and point out different stocks as the ticker tape raced by. His major piece of advice: "Beth Ann, never invest more than you can afford to lose."

The new Dean Witter Reynolds office opened in August of 1984 and it was beautiful. There were around thirty-five new brokers, only two of which were women. Each sales assistant was assigned five brokers to answer their phones and send out all of their mailings. Starting wage was $5.75 an hour. The work was occasionally exciting when the market was on a bounce, but was mostly mundane secretarial work. I did have a few of the office misfits on my team who made things interesting. They would fall out of favor with the manager when they were late showing up for work. I needed more stimulation. Several of us asked to get sponsorship started and began studying the course material. Each chapter had an exam that followed. I was called into the manager's office shortly after.

"Beth, you're really doing a good job keeping up with the brokers' work."

"I try to be organized, that's all."

"Well, the reason I called you in is we've decided to give you another team of brokers, so you'll be following ten instead of five of them."

Oh, joy I thought – that's what efficiency will get you. There was no mention of a pay raise even though I was expected to handle double the work of other assistants. Pretty soon, the brokers were asking me about ten dollar stocks and twelve dollar stocks I'd been following that I would occasionally purchase. I asked for a raise and my pay was increased a quarter an hour. I began buying the Wall Street Journal on the way to the office. The only place that carried it near my home was in an adult book store, so I'd shake them up in the morning strutting in the door wearing a suit and heels. I had worked myself into being the market and research assistant for ten brokers. After almost a year, I was granted a raise to $6.75 an hour.

Still, I felt I needed something more physical to do, so I interviewed for a spot in a night class on massage therapy. A nurse named Carl from Traverse City was going to drive down twice weekly to teach the course. There were ten spots in the class and he said there were one hundred and four applicants. He had interviews scheduled all afternoon the day I was to meet him.

"Beth, why should I choose you to be one of the ten students? You aren't in the medical field or physical therapy and I have over a hundred candidates. Why should I give you a spot in the class?"

I looked him straight in the eye and replied, "Because I've got the touch."

"So you've got the touch."

"Yes . . . that's it . . . I've got the touch."

I think curiosity convinced him to let me in the class and all of us had a great time in the months of training. We all had to do one hundred hours of internship for the course, so many of our clients were given free massages at the WMCA where classes were held. Some were boxers; others were basketball players and even housewives with sore backs or necks. Part of our final exam was giving our instructor a partial massage. He would quiz you while the massage was in progress. When it was my turn, I worked on his upper back as he rattled off questions regarding the different muscle areas. He stopped me after less than ten minutes.

"That's it . . . you pass . . . and yes, you've definitely got <u>the touch</u>."

I was pleased and told him thanks for taking a chance on me. In the months that followed, I worked on brokers with stiff necks from doing cold calling on the phones, and spent a few evenings and Saturdays as a therapist at a high-end salon in Farmington Hills.

A few months later, I was asked to help out with the new group of massage therapy students. Carl, the instructor had become quite popular as a teacher. What I hadn't known was that he had been the boxer's personal massage therapist to Tommy "the hit man" Hearns.

Carl came to me and told me about his new dilemma. Tommy Hearns had a big fight coming up and he wanted Carl with him while he trained for three weeks in Florida, then to spend one week in Las Vegas for the fight.

"Beth, I just can't go, not in the middle of all my classes. Tommy asked if there was someone good I could recommend and I told him about you. I'd like you to meet with him. He's invited us to the Detroit Yacht Club on Saturday if that will work for you."

And that we did. The three of us had lunch and Tommy was pretty clear about the responsibilities. I had done massages on boxers at the YMCA and it is truly a workout for the therapist, too. I told him that I'd have to check and see if my manager at Dean Witter would let me go away for a month without jeopardizing my job. My manager was kind, but said no, that my ten brokers needed me more. So much for that pipedream – travel, excitement, and good pay would have to wait. I stayed put.

Then, calamity struck at work. Apparently our manager displeased his organization and was removed and sent to another office. It had to do with one of the female brokers and it had gotten messy due to too much 'togetherness." Our new manager, a young guy in his thirties, called each of the market assistants studying for the Series 7 Exam into his office one by one. We methodically got the same speech.

"So, you think you'd like to be a stockbroker, eh? Well, I don't think so. I don't believe women are suited for this business, so I'd like you to gather together your study materials and return them to the office tomorrow. We will no longer be sponsoring you."

I was incensed. Who did he think he was? I was already halfway through the course. One by one, we came out of his office totally disgusted. There was really no protection that we knew of then regarding workplace discrimination. Obviously, this guy wasn't paying much attention in managerial classes. It's got to be in the top five of what not to do and that is, "Do not aggravate, irritate, or piss off the majority of your support staff, especially all in the same day." At a pow-wow we had after work, three of us each wrote out letters of resignation and turned them in the next day with our study packets. I had nearly worked there a year to the day. It was back to job hunting once again.

My brother, Brad was a glazier, a fancy name for a glass installer and told me the unions had discussed minority hiring in that field and that I should apply. I was ready to try anything and Brad was good. I knew I could learn a lot from him and maybe eventually we could work together in the field. In the meantime, I had already tested to get into skilled trades at General Motors, worked as a perfume demonstrator at Hudson's, a process server for a law firm, and a food demonstrator at local supermarkets while looking for something substantial.

The glass company Brad worked for was in Pontiac and not in a terrific neighborhood. I went in to see his boss at least three times. I guess the third time was when he weakened.

"I won't even consider putting you to work in the field—no way. It's hard enough to get these guys to concentrate on their work without putting you in the mix. Maybe we could use you in the office."

I wasn't nuts about the idea, but I was hired "for the office" and started at $5.75 an hour. He already employed a very territorial secretary who had a death grip on anything in the office that I was more than qualified to do. One day, the boss sent me out in his luxury car to deliver paychecks to the different construction sites. I also was instructed to pick up his dry cleaning, his carryout lunch, and other odd jobs. Once a month, I'd give him a haircut which was his "perk" for having me there. He did have great hair.

Then, I saw an advertisement in the newspaper for a company called Troy Design Services. We arranged an interview which went well, and a few weeks later they sent me to General Motors Engineering to interview for an expediter position. A very nice man named Jim managed the area and hired me and also gave me a large increase in pay. Then there was an opportunity to become a member of the Quality Survey Team for GM. I was asked to join their team touring facilities that were producing our prototype truck parts. I remained on the team for a couple of years. Eventually, I was given the opportunity to move into a process engineering position, in charge of some of the prototype truck builds.

My high school auto mechanics classes served me well and came in handy after all. I had been the first girl in the history of Waterford Township High School to take auto mechanics which nearly drove Norm, the teacher nuts. But if you asked him, I believe he'd tell you that I was a pretty darn good mechanic. I even sewed lace on the pocket of my work jumpsuit to get his goat. It stopped him mid-sentence one day and he just shook his head.

But, I still maintained a presence in therapeutic massage. One day, I met a man named Mark who told me about a friend of his that was an AP mechanic at the Oakland Pontiac Airport. His name was Gary; he owned his own plane and was in desperate need of relief from a chronic back problem. Hours of lying underneath a plane played havoc with his condition. After an introduction at the airport I agreed to work on his back and see if it would relieve his pain. Gary's father had been a pilot and had owned a hanger at the airport. He later died in a plane crash.

Massage therapy actually did help and Gary was very grateful. We agreed to barter massage therapy for flying lessons. I had never been in a small plane before. He set me up with a fellow who flew freight as well as Lear jets and he would be my first instructor.

The day of my first lesson, I went through the checklist; inspecting the plane, checking it externally and internally and making sure it had adequate gas in it. He explained the inner workings, the gauges, brakes, flaps, wind speed and still, I was really interested in something I thought was missing.

"Hey, I'm curious . . . where's the parachutes?"

"No parachutes in a plane with a heavily populated area. If the plane goes down, you go down with it."

"You're kidding, right?"

"No . . . I'm not."

"Oh . . . well . . . okay, let's get started."

That very first day, it was a combination of fear and euphoria in taking off, up and away into the sky in the little puddle jumper, with no parachute to salvage my life. We flew for about half an hour. The next sentence out of the pilot's mouth gave me pause.

"Well, you caught on to flying very quickly, so I'm going to have you land the plane. Please stay on the runway and out of the grass or you'll embarrass me."

What? Was he kidding? Land the plane on my very first day? Was he crazy or was I? But, I was able to land the plane just fine. I was so proud of myself. After that, I was hooked. Each time Gary would maintenance a plane I asked him to call me and I'd be at the airport in a matter of minutes and have him take me up with him. I wanted to fly in as many planes as I could. It was a blast. Later, we would fly to Osh Kosh, Wisconsin for the International Air Shows and make a few trips to Florida and back with his sister Gail and brother-in-law, Morrey. Morrey had flown in three wars and definitely was a seasoned pilot as was his wife. We had just had the best of times. The freedom of flying was incredible. Gary and I dated for some time, and I considered buying a small plane for sale at the airport. But, while taking flying lessons, I developed an irregular heartbeat and was grounded later by my doctor until we could find the cause of it. Gary and I parted ways, and then being a plane owner seemed a little out of reach. I do have great memories of all of our flights, even the one flying around a tornado.

Chapter 47

THE BLUE RIVIERA

In 1988, and at thirty-eight years old, I decided I was ready for a different car. I had purchased my father's 1984 Pontiac Fiero from him a few years earlier. It had been a fun car, but it was treacherous driving it in the winter. I felt like I was behind the wheel of a runaway roller skate with a mind of its own. I decided to take a day off work and go car hunting. I would visit nine dealerships that day, searching for either a 1984 Buick Riviera or a Cadillac Eldorado. I loved the body style and wanted a little luxury to go with it. The fourth dealership I visited was on Dixie Highway and had a beautiful blue Riviera on the used car lot. The salesman told me that it had belonged to a doctor that bought a new one. It was a pretty car with a small amount of rust surfacing on trim pieces on the rear quarter panels. I decided to make the rounds and see what else was out there. In spite of the salesman urging me to leave a deposit, I waved goodbye and told him I may be back. He stood in the lot giving me that dejected look.

After stops that encompassed the rest of my afternoon, there was no other car that caught my fancy. I stopped back by that evening and left a deposit for the Riviera. My father offered to drive me to the dealership the following day to pick the car up. I was paying cash for it, so there would be very little paperwork. Working at GM had afforded me a good living, and it had been easy to squirrel away the money. We were led to a cubicle in the used car section, one that was wood from the floor up three or four feet, then clear glass up four more feet. Dad and I sat down across from one another waiting for my salesman to return with the papers. Suddenly, a foreboding feeling washed over me, leaving me very ill at ease.

"Beth, what's wrong? You look sick. You got so pale."

"I feel like someone is staring at me."

I felt the hair on the back of my neck stand up. There is something to be said for intuition.

"There is . . . a man standing behind you in the next booth is staring over here."

As I slowly turned to see who was causing me this discomfort, the sight of him sucked the breath right out of me. It was the man who had raped me in 1977.

"That's him, Dad. That's the man that put me in the hospital when Ray and I were separated. That's the man who raped me."

Suddenly, I didn't care about a car or anything else. I just wanted to get out of there as quickly as possible. A new wave of nausea began to take over. I stood up just as my salesman appeared.

"Well, folks, here's all your papers and your new set of car keys, young lady," my salesman said, laying everything out on the table. He handed me a pen and I could barely write my name.

"What's with that man who's standing in the next booth? He keeps staring," I said coldly.

"Oh, that's Tom, the used car manager. He's harmless," he answered, chuckling.

Now I had a new concern. He had all of my personal information: my address and phone number, license plate number and car description, even where I worked. In the months to come, I had the car repainted and the minor rust spots refurbished. But, I just couldn't shake the memories and that one day brought it all back. In less than eighteen months I sold the car.

Chapter 48

CAREER CLATTER

In the late 1980's, GM was still a wonderful place to work until Jim, my manager left our department and was replaced by a high-level female. She dressed the part and I believed that she could have been a decent supervisor if she hadn't felt the need to constantly compete with the other females in the office for attention. If a high-level gentleman in GM spoke to one of us, she felt she was being ignored and we'd pay dearly for it. She demonstrated the need to belittle others to make herself feel better. It had become a terrible work environment. I felt tremendous pressure each day and began having an irregular heartbeat (yes, the same kind that grounded me from flying). One day my heart rhythm got so bad causing a hard, painful thumping in my chest that I stopped at the local fire department where my brother, Tom was a fireman-paramedic.

"Tom, there's something not right going on with my heart. It's got a wacky beat and it's starting to make my chest sore. Can you connect me to your portable EKG machine so I can see the rhythm?"

I thought if I saw it on paper I may recognize what it was doing from my years working for the cardiologists. I thought my brother might be able to help, too.

"Okay, hop in the back of this rig. Let's hook you up and I'll run a rhythm strip."

He ran a very long strip on graph paper and began studying it. I saw this look of concern on his face. Then he opened the back of the rig and jumped out, saying he wanted to let a couple other paramedics take a look. It all made me nervous. He was back within two minutes.

"Beth, I showed the guys and they said if we had a patient showing that rhythm, we'd be sending them to the hospital."

"Well, maybe I better call Dr. K and tell him what it shows and see what he thinks."

I was concerned. Dr. K was more concerned.

"Beth, I want you to go into Emergency. I'm going to call and tell them you're on your way. There are a few things we need to check out now. I'll talk to you later, okay? I'll have one of my residents take good care of you."

I drove myself to the hospital, which I don't recommend, but my brother couldn't leave work. They immediately put me on bed rest, a heart monitor, started an I.V., and put me on medications for a condition called bigeminy. I called my family, but they were busy having dinner at my sister's house. Dr. K had the resident physician tell me why he sent me into the hospital. There was a possibility of a blood clot in the heart. I was there over fourteen hours. The doctor said I should stay overnight, but I promised to see a cardiologist in Dr. K's office in the morning. The following day, I had an echocardiogram and a few other tests. When things were sorted out as far as the test results, the doctor was very blunt.

"When I see this condition, it's pretty much the same in ninety percent of the cases, especially when it affects women. This is generally caused by stress. When you remove the source of the stress, the condition usually goes away. By what you've told me, you need to quit your job."

"Oh, really? And when would you and your wife like me to move in?"

He chuckled. I was serious; I had to make a living here. I left his office and began to think about what I should do with my life. It was time to examine what I had enjoyed doing the most. I really liked real estate and being my own boss. I just hated working Sundays. I enjoyed taking care of patients when I worked for Dr. K, but I dead-ended myself, lacking in education and a degree. This was the opportune time to make a plan to change my life. I didn't really feel I was doing much for mankind by supervising prototype truck builds, anyway. Besides, it was time to think more about this stress issue and my own health.

I decided to start by taking a college course or two with a goal in mind and see if it agreed with me. I'd already taken Business Law in 1985, which had been taught by a local judge and had been purely for my own satisfaction. I knew a college degree would take much more dedication. Saving money was imperative for tuition and books, so I continued at GM while I positioned myself for change. My manager could barely get me rattled now. I had a plan, and I had already mentally started "leaving the building" so to speak. I interviewed and was granted a part-time position working evenings at the Palace of Auburn Hills, a large entertainment venue as a Suite Captain in corporate suites after I got off work from GM. There, I was fitted for a tuxedo, a 36 regular. Then I went to a local salon where my friend, Kip worked part-time and I agreed to work every Saturday there doing massage therapy or cutting hair – whatever was needed. I knew a bankroll would be necessary for my new adventure to become reality.

Chapter 49

A HANDSOME AFTER-WORK SURPRISE

It was a night to remember in the summer of 1988. I had worked at the Palace that Friday night. There was a heavy metal band that performed and I could hardly wait for the concert to end. I was much more of a cool jazz type. Quickly changing out of my tux, I was ready to go outside and get some air; it had been an obnoxious crowd to put up with. My nerves were jangled as I waited and waited to get out of the parking lot. Heading for home, I still couldn't relax, so I turned into the entrance of a local dance bar. Dancing was pretty much a cure for everything. Maybe I'll dance a little, have a drink and head for home. It seemed like a logical way to get ready for sleep.

After getting a vodka and tonic, I headed to the edge of the dance floor where I was pretty good spotting the guys that were really into dancing like I was. It was such a great pleasure to be listening to a good song with a thumping beat compared to what I had just left; it was one of the good memories from earlier days as a disc jockey. I was smiling when a man standing nearby leaned in and spoke to me.

"It's been a pretty nice crowd tonight. When did you get here?"

"A few minutes ago – I just came from work."

"Gee, you must work late. It's after one a.m. "

He was strikingly handsome, with black hair and brown eyes, and I loved his red shirt and his stylish white leather shoes. If a man takes care of his shoes, he generally takes good care of himself and his environment. I decided to finish my drink quickly. I wanted to dance with him and I wasn't going to sit my drink down for even a second – it was just too risky.

"I worked at the Palace tonight. The concert was too raucous for me. I thought if I danced a couple dances, I'd be able to relax. Are you up for it?"

"Sure," he answered. We talked and danced until closing time. I later recalled being introduced to him five years earlier by one of the cosmetology students where I went to school. She had such a crush on him, and as good friends should, I steered clear of him.

Tonight, however, was going to be different. I'd find out if he was attached, engaged, or involved before I spent too much time. It turned out his name was Gil, divorced and no attachments.

"If you're not too tired, would you be up for having breakfast with me?" he asked, grinning.

"I'd like that. You know, I haven't gone out for breakfast this late since I was in my twenties."

It was a beautiful night for it. The air was balmy and there were lots of stars visible in the night sky. We sat slowly sipping coffee and eating hash browns and eggs in a nearby all-night restaurant. And after that night, we were hardly ever apart. He worked in one of the GM plants about five miles from my engineering building and he lived in Waterford too, less than three miles from my house. How it was that we never even crossed paths from grocery stores to gas stations I couldn't fathom. Then my mind flashed back to a conversation I had with my mother not a month earlier.

"You know, Mom, I've actually reached a point that I'm pretty contented with my life and I'll be okay if I never get married again."

"I'm glad, honey," she answered, almost relieved. What a difference a day would make.

Chapter 50

ANOTHER TRY AT LOVE

Gil and I began seeing so much of each other that we began to wonder why we kept two homes. Mine was a small two bedroom near the lake where I kept my pontoon boat; his was an older brick story and a half with an in-ground pool and a large lot. I was thirty-eight years old and I'd never been interested in living with a man outside of marriage; it just wasn't for me.

One evening while at his place, I looked him in the eye and asked if he was really serious about me. He seemed surprised, then walked over to his desk and retrieved a picture to show me. It was beautiful engagement ring. I felt like I may have spoiled it for him, but I was very happy just the same. We began talking about the future and decided to get married in August, a year after we met. In the course of our many conversations I had always felt the need to practically apologize for being married and divorced twice. I knew it was a sticking point with some men. He never said anything positive or negative about it in particular, but just listened in silence.

We decided to celebrate our engagement by taking a trip to Mexico together in March of 1989. Winters in Michigan didn't seem so long with a trip to a warm place during the winter months. It was a survival skill to me. I was so focused on the trip that I nearly ignored a troublesome occurrence. My hands and forearms were feeling numb one minute, prickly the next. I was constantly using a computer keyboard at work for long stretches and wondered if I was getting carpal tunnel syndrome or something related to the vertebrae in my neck. I made an appointment with a neurologist not far from my office. The soonest appointment was the day before we were to fly to Mexico.

Dr. G had a nice office with friendly staff. When he came in to see me, he was quite charming when he walked through the door. I was stunned at what he said after the brief amount of small talk.

"Doctor, I'm really concerned. I've been having this strange numbness and tingling in my arms. I work with computers most of my workday. Do you think it's related to my work? I'm leaving on a trip to Mexico tomorrow with my fiancé and wonder what you think it might be causing it."

"Engaged? What did you want to go and do that for? Come on, you really don't want to get married. If you break your engagement you could go out with someone . . . like me, for instance."

"No, that won't be happening. I'm very happy."

With that, his demeanor changed. He began testing my reflexes and quickly finished. I think he was in the room a mere five minutes or so.

"Well, I think you have multiple sclerosis. There's nothing you can do about it. Go ahead and take your trip to Mexico. It might be the last trip you'll be able to take, so enjoy." With that, he left the room. Was it blatant sarcasm or a reaction to feeling some rejection? I had no idea.

I wasn't expecting anything even close to his words – it was incredibly depressing news. A friend of mine's father had M.S. and was confined to bed, paralyzed from the neck down. It appeared as if he was merely existing and not really living. It seemed so dismal. I didn't know what to say or do. I was emotionally numb when I left the office. It stuck in my mind that this doctor used extremely poor judgment in pulling the flirtation card during such a serious conversation.

The next day, Gil and I were on our way to Mexico. Time and time again, I felt conflicted. I began nervously twirling my engagement ring on my finger. The plane ride seemed like an eternity, nearly claustrophobic. My mind raced . . . why would a doctor make a claim like that without running any tests first? Do I keep it to myself or share it? Should I break our engagement and give him back the ring now? Would he even still want me if I turned out to be "damaged goods?"

"Gil . . . I've been thinking . . . um, I'm, well . . ."

"Well . . . what?" he said as he looked over at me inquisitively and squeezed my hand.

"It's just . . . well, I'm hoping it's really warm when we get to Mexico."

I chickened out. I didn't want to lose him. The trip progressed as planned; comfortable room, good food, and beautiful weather until a visit one afternoon to a popular restaurant that had its restrooms upstairs, only reachable by using a spiral staircase. My legs ached going up and on the way down, my left leg gave out and I began tumbling down the swirling iron stairway. It was humiliating. I tried to stay composed, but the words out of that doctor's mouth echoed in my brain and I tried not to sob as Gil helped me up. I swore that very minute I would prove the jerk doctor wrong.

Thankfully, the remainder of the trip was enjoyable and relaxing – just what the doctor ordered, right? In the meantime, bruises began to surface on my left side, arm and hand. I made an appointment with another neurologist, Dr. E, for March 24, 1989. By mid-March the symptoms had moved to my left ribcage, leaving me breathless and in pain during my gym workouts, eventually spreading into my abdomen. Then more bruising surfaced in the left hip and thigh. The neurologist ordered a VER, brain stem test, an MRI and labs. I began seeing a chiropractor, Dr. G and felt somewhat better. Then I started spotting blood in my urine. I began anxiously awaiting my return appointment to get the test results from Dr. E. I asked Gil if he'd go with me for the results thinking that we might as well find out together.

"Well, you definitely don't have M.S. My feeling is that it's a virus, it's self-limiting and all of your symptoms should be gone in three to four months. That's it."

There was no more explanation than that. My feeling of relief was profound; my gratitude real. I was given another chance at getting what I really wanted – to be happy loving someone and being loved in return. The symptoms did subside and then magically disappeared. I attacked college with more zest and looked forward to the future.

Chapter 51

MARRIAGE, MOVING ON, AND MOVING OVER

On August 9, 1989, Gil and I agreed to meet at the Oakland County Courthouse to apply for our marriage license. That department must be one of the most interesting perches as a people-watching place for seeing and hearing almost anything and everything. We were giddy standing in line waiting for our turn at the window after filling out the necessary forms.

"So, Miss Griffin, I see that you've been married twice, is that right?"

"Yes, I'm afraid so," I admitted, looking down at the floor.

"And Sir, I see that you've also been married twice?"

"Uh, well, uh, yes, that's right," Gil answered quickly glancing at me.

I held up a finger motioning "just a moment" to the lady at the window. I took Gil's arm and walked briskly over toward the outer hallway.

"What's that? Is that true, Gil? You've been married twice before just like I have? When were you planning on telling me? You've listened to me apologize all over the place about being married twice and you've said nothing! How do you think that makes me feel, especially to not find out until this very minute? If you'd keep that from me, are there more things I'm going to 'stumble' across? I'm sorry, but I'm out of here – we're done here."

"Wait, Beth. Please, don't be mad at me . . . it's no big deal. Come on."

"It is a big deal, Gil. Why would you leave out a 'little thing' like a marriage? What else aren't you telling me? It involves honesty and trust. I can't do this. The wedding's off."

I stormed out of the building, got in my car and drove away as he stood on the sidewalk. I swore that I was not going to feel like a fool again because of a man. As that feeling of vulnerability crept back in, I quickly withdrew into my emotional shell and we didn't speak again for days. But then I began to really miss him. We'd hardly been apart in months.

Only after great consternation and much soul-searching did we reconcile and head back to the courthouse one last time. We were married on August 25, 1989 at the Waterford Township Courthouse by a magistrate. Mom was my matron of honor. We had both families join us at The Pike Street Company Restaurant for a celebration dinner, and then left the following night for a honeymoon in Spain.

Spain was a wonderful change of pace. Gil had been there before and was excited for me to experience it. Siesta every day from noon to three o'clock was a refreshing respite, but having dinner after ten in the evening proved to be a challenge. The restaurants were relatively empty until then. Entire families would be out in the streets at midnight, eating at the open air cafes.

It was puzzling though, to walk down a crowded street and have people part to let us by without saying a word. Some days during siesta, we'd channel surf and their television programs were heavy with soap operas in Spanish. I began looking at the actors wondering if Gil resembled one of them. There was no match. The fourth day there I finally got the answer. As we meandered through an open air market, a middle-aged woman with flowing black hair stepped back, as she uttered a few words in English. I doubled back to speak to her.

"Why do they step back when this man passes?" I asked curiously.

"Because we know who he is. He is famous . . . a bullfighter from Madrid."

We chuckled over it, especially since Gil barely spoke any Spanish. He told me that when he attended school at five years of age, he only spoke Spanish because that's all that was spoken in his home. Kids made fun of him and he vowed never to be teased over it again. He admitted to having forgotten much more Spanish than he remembered.

My brother John had purchased my home. When we returned, Gil and I began living under his roof and we began remodeling the house. I soon discovered working in carpentry and home renovation suited me. We enjoyed working together on most everything. It's the happiest I'd been in a long time. Moving him over to give me some mattress at night, now that was a challenge.

Chapter 52

PAINFUL NEWS FOR GRADUATION

In 1990 and at forty years old, I left General Motors for good. While taking some of my college courses, I began doing part-time work as a nurse aide for a home health staffing company. Some of my patients were wealthy and living in beautiful homes but were losing the battle with their health. Others lived in house trailers and low income apartments. One patient of mine was a brave young man who became a quadriplegic after a fall from a tree when he was twelve. He had learned to do many things by holding a pointer in his mouth and landed a job in admissions at the local college. It was the only thing he could hold. He was so inspiring and never complained. You couldn't help but feel blessed to have known him.

College for me was no breeze. I had to be very disciplined and driven, finding it harder than I had imagined. After my prerequisite classes were completed, the remaining two years were nursing rotations and the advanced courses leading to graduation. My study cards were illustrated color coded four by six cards that I could carry to the gym and study from while I did laps on the track. Dinner was on the table no later than five. Dishes were off the table and done by six. Study period was six p.m. to nine p.m. each weeknight. My brain seemed to sense it when the clock struck nine and would shift into hibernation. It didn't take long to realize I had to give up trying to stuff one more morsel of information into my head. Then Gil and I would relax, curling up together to watch a little television. That was the rhythm of things.

In 1993, during the last year of college, we sold our house and moved to an older ranch home in Bloomfield Hills. It was previously owned by a rather tall couple and they had their counters and vanities all raised in the house to even out the height difference. The oven literally was sitting on the kitchen countertop so the wife didn't have to bend over to remove things. It was an odd site. Gil saw it as a challenge and I liked the neighborhood and the beautiful backyard, so we bought it and began remodeling the kitchen immediately. I would cook with a microwave and a portable two-burner cook top for the next two years. At school I became involved in campus photography, was asked to join the Dean's Council, became a member of the Honors Students, and was nominated for Nursing Student of the Year by one of my instructors. That spring while I studied for final exams, prepped for Nursing State Boards, completed my final issues paper, interviewed for nursing positions and anticipated the upcoming graduation ceremonies, I slipped into a state of indescribable pain. This wasn't numbness or a prickly feeling – it felt as if someone was holding my legs in front of a blow torch scorching them over and over and it was agonizing. The discomfort had started in February of 1993 when I slipped while outdoors shaking rugs. There was no fall, but within two days my left side began to violently itch, and then numbness to the left of my spine which followed the nerve pathway around to the front of my body. There was a tightness there that caused my left lower abdomen to feel as though my intestines were tied into tight knots.

In the next three months I would see Dr. G, an endearing and really good chiropractor; Dan, a very learned physical therapist; and Dr. W, a gynecologist to rule out an abdominal mass. Then, back to see Dr. R, my original orthopedic surgeon from 1968, and finally returning to Dr. E, the neurologist. I'd never been one to run to a doctor so all of this seemed so foreign to me. No one seemed to know what was causing it. Dr. E was booked up but had a cancellation on April 9th. That day I was put on the medication Lioresal to take up to four times a day for pain and then was scheduled to have an MRI done on April 13th. By the day after the test, the pain was nearly off the charts. I called Dr. E crying, begging for some relief.

"This medicine is just not working. I'm on a break from a lecture in class and I can't sit still because this wrenching pain is so bad," I choked out the words while sobbing into the phone.

"Are you trying visual imagery and meditation?"

"I'm long past all that. Listen, Doctor, this pain is incredible. I can't concentrate."

"Well, you haven't been on the medication long enough to see if it will work. Just try it for five more days. If there's no relief, I'll give you something else."

190

On April 18th, I called Dr. E's office again for a medication change – this stuff was just not helping at all. I was told she left on vacation and wouldn't be back until April 30th and to call the office back in the morning. I stayed up most of the night pacing. I reached the office the following day from a college corridor.

"Who's covering for Dr. E while she's gone?"

"Another doctor here is."

"Well, tell him I waited the additional five days and the medication isn't working. It's been long enough! I NEED SOMETHING ELSE and I want my MRI results."

"We'll call you in something for pain but no, you can't have the results – not until your doctor returns. It's against our policy to give test results for other doctors."

"So I have to wait eleven more days? You've <u>got</u> to be kidding! Do you have any idea how much this is messing up my life right now? I'm in college. I have college finals and State Boards. I'm in severe pain. Does this mean anything to you people?"

I was livid, then frantic. I called my orthopedic doctor back and he said he'd get the results for me. At least his office was trying to help. In the meantime, two more days passed before any prescription was called in by Dr. E's fill-in doctor to my pharmacy. I think I called their office ten times in two days. This lack of compassion in medicine began to trouble me.

Dr. R's office called me on April 22nd. Thank God, <u>he</u> was a man of his word.

"Didn't the hospital call you? They said they wanted you to come back and have the MRI repeated."

"No, they never called me. Why? They didn't say <u>why</u> I need another MRI?"

"Nope – just that a doctor there wanted a few more views and you shouldn't have to be in that machine too long."

I called the hospital that day. They told me they'd left a message on my answering machine. There wasn't one. I was told to never mind the message – that there was a cancellation and I could have the MRI done that night. Meanwhile, the Tylenol with codeine that was ordered for me was making me very sick to my stomach. I stopped it. I knew I'd need to take some Ativan before the MRI; it's ordered for the claustrophobia that's caused from being inside such a small cylinder. It's like being pushed into a driveway culvert and left there for God knows how long. The Ativan hadn't kicked in when I was taken back for the test. I hyperventilated and thought I was going to throw up in the machine. They pulled me out, gave me a moment and a sip of water and I asked that Gil be able to stay in the room and hold onto my foot. Just knowing there is someone out there lessens that panicky feeling. When the test was completed I made sure Dr. R's name was down to receive the test results. He called the following day on April 23rd.

"Well, you've got a long cyst off the spinal cord called a syrinx. It looks like you'll need to see a neurosurgeon." He suggested one and then called him. My final exams were in just three days. My sister, Terry had given me some Darvocct to try to get me through my exams. I just hoped that it wouldn't make me too groggy; I needed to be able to think straight.

Finally, my last final exam was over. I sat still as everyone left the classroom so that I could lag behind and get a chance to talk to Mrs. S. She had been a wonderful instructor and I'd grown to appreciate her so much.

"Got a minute?"

"Sure . . . say, you don't look like you're feeling well. Is everything okay?"

"Well, that's why I wanted to talk to you. I've been having horrific pain in my left side and back and it's been a long ordeal finding out what's been causing it. I just got the MRI test results. Who would you see if you needed spinal surgery?"

Then I handed her the MRI report. She quickly read through it and then sat gazing ahead.

"Did you know that our Dean of Nursing's husband is a physician? I'd talk to him. He's a neuroradiologist and he would know."

Later she got him on the phone and read him my report. He said that this condition was complicated and I should get to a big medical center. He also said that if I could get my MRI films to him through his wife, he would take them to his hospital and get a thorough look. I picked up the films the following day and ran them out to the college to the Dean of Nursing. It was only the second time I had been in her office. The first time was a month or so earlier when I was summoned to her office, the reason unknown. When I arrived I thought I was in some kind of trouble.

"Actually, I wanted to speak with you in private, Beth. I've heard a lot of good things about you and would like you to consider continuing your education to obtain your Masters degree. There's a good transitional program at Wayne State University and it would make me very happy to have you come and teach here at the College in the nursing program. Would you be interested? "

"I'm really honored that you'd even ask, but I've grown pretty weary of school at the moment and I just need to take a break from it. I will give it some thought, though. Thank you so much for asking."

I'm sure that it was a surprise to have me back in her office in less than a month and under such different circumstances. In the meantime, Dr. R suggested a local neurologist, Dr. C and arranged an appointment for me. Gil went with me on April 27th. The doctor asked that I not take any pain medications that day. The trip up the stairs proved to be slow and painful. Dr. C studied the films and said the "syringomyelia," was very visible and there were further tests I should have performed but said the condition was out of his league and it should be addressed by a major medical center. Then he gave me a prescription for Vicodin.

On April 28th, The Dean of Nursing and her husband called and asked if Gil and I would come over that evening for tea. It must be news, I thought. Within an hour we were sitting in their living room.

"Beth, I'm curious . . . this condition can be caused from being in an accident, like a high-speed crash. Were you ever in an accident like that?"

"I was in a head-on collision when I was seventeen, but my injuries turned out to be minor. I had been in the back seat and was thrown under the driver's seat on impact."

"I want you to see Dr. M . . . it's who I would go to with something like this. You'd benefit from having a myelogram which would give a clearer picture of what you're dealing with."

They were both so kind. I thanked them for their time, took my MRI films back and Gil and I left for home.

In the meantime, I knew I'd have to let my new employer know that my start date would need to be delayed so I could get these tests and appointments out of the way. I had secured a position as a staff RN in an inner city hospital in the E.R. The head of the emergency room agreed to give me until June 14th to wrap things up. I knew it was important to be up front about it. I couldn't work doped up on painkillers.

On May 4th, Mom accompanied me to Henry Ford Hospital to see the neurosurgeon, Dr. M, that the Dean's husband recommended. He was very direct.

"Beth, I'm not recommending surgery. There's a possibility that it may correct itself by the fibers splitting. I don't think surgery is wise. If you were in a wheelchair, it would be different, but surgery for this could end up putting you in a wheelchair. It's just too risky. I'd like to get you in to see a neurologist here at this hospital."

Another neurologist was not what I wanted to hear. I had begun to feel like a ping pong ball. He recommended another Dr. E that was available to see me that morning. After the exam, Mom came back into the room as the doctor slid into a chair and sat staring at me before finally speaking.

"Do you really feel it's necessary to know what this is? I'm asking, because once the diagnosis is officially made and if it's bad, it will jeopardize you getting work and health insurance. And your previous doctor that saw you four years ago should not have told you it wasn't multiple sclerosis because it wasn't proven."

"Yes, Doctor, it is important to me. I would never have gone back to college to get a nursing degree if this was even a possibility. I would have returned to real estate. And now, to even think about going after a BSN or a Masters degree – what would you do if you were in my shoes? Wouldn't you want to know?"

Then there was silence – nothing but silence. He took me off all painkillers on May 5th and started me on Elavil for the leg spasms, casually mentioning the medicine may take two to six weeks to show any effectiveness.

On May 7th, the day of my nursing graduation pinning ceremony, the pain resurfaced with a vengeance. I called Dr. E's office asking if it was possible to take some Vicodin and that I wanted to get my blood test results. The doctor's nurse, Carol took the message and asked what time the ceremony was to be held and they would get back with me between 11:30 and 12:30. I was lying on the floor next to the phone at 3:30 p.m., crying from the pain when Gill got home from work.

"Gil, I just can't go. I'm not going to be able to stand it. I'm in too much pain."

Gil was irate and called their office, getting an answering machine. He was yelling into the phone that someone better do something. The phone rang back within a minute. It was Dr. E.

"Just for today you can take some Vicodin. Take the Elavil tonight. Have a good time."

I took some Vicodin and we rushed out the door heading to the campus. My legs began to turn to rubber. During the ceremony, we had to climb the steps to the stage and walk across to receive our nursing pins. I was buzzed. I said a quick prayer that I not trip and fall face first on center stage.

On May 10th, I called Dr. E's office to get my test results back: MRI, VEP, SSEP, and blood tests. Carol was very nasty on the phone and told me the first opening for an appointment was in July.

"Carol, I can't wait two months for my results."

"Well, there's nothing I can do about it."

"I'd like a phone call from Dr. E. – when will he be in next?"

"On Thursday."

"Would you have him please call me Thursday?"

"No . . . if you want him to call you Thursday, you'll have to call back Thursday and ask again."

Now, I'm ready to hurt this woman. What an absolute bitch. I called Dr. B who had sent me to him in the first place and told him what a terrible time I was having dealing with his office. Dr. B got my MRI results and read it to me. It showed some demyelination consistent with M.S. in addition to the syrinx. He then asked when I'd be seeing Dr. E. I told him the first appointment I could get was "in July." He called Dr. E himself. Then I finally got a call back. I was told to be at Dr. E's office at 9:00 a.m. the next day – that things were "complicated" and he thought we should talk in person. I guess he didn't know that the cat was already out of the bag.

Gil and I went together the following day, May 15th. We could have skipped it. I already knew what I needed to know. I would not be returning to college. I was going to stop seeing Dr. E and

195

his tempestuous and bitchy office staff. I was done with all the drama. My life would go on. I would eventually meet an interesting and passionate neurologist at my new job. He was a godsend. Dr. M's attitude was positive and treatment was simple – two medications and the use of an old saying, "if it ain't broke, don't fix it." I saw him about once a year over the next ten years and only ended up switching doctors because he killed himself.

Chapter 53

A STUNT UNAVENGED

Many Sunday afternoons after having breakfast out, Gil and I were "regulars" shopping the home improvement stores and building centers in the area. The house renovation was a continuing project, spreading out into the backyard. It would include a new deck which Gil designed and we planned to build it together. One beautiful Sunday afternoon, after having a large breakfast and many cups of coffee, we were once again walking the aisles in one of those stores.

"Gil, I'm running to the restroom . . . I drank too much coffee today."

As I made my way to the back of the store, the hallway leading to the bathrooms took me past the employee break room. There was a window in the break room door and I noticed a few people inside buying snacks from the vending machines. Once in the empty women's bathroom, I stepped into a stall and sat down. Then I heard the bathroom door open. It's very common to glance down and watch a pair of shoes pass by. Curiously, I saw no feet.

Scarcely a second had passed when I was suddenly jerked off the toilet by my ankles, my pants hanging down below my knees. I only saw the man's hands, arms and the sleeves of his shirt. His skin was a dark tan color, his knuckles were covered in black hair, and the shirt was green, black and white flannel plaid. He was trying to pull me part way under the door which blocked any view of his face. I began grabbing at the toilet paper dispenser, desperately trying to hold onto anything. It tore loose off the wall. I tried to scream and barely a noise came out of my mouth. I kept trying to kick him, but his grip was strong. I wouldn't let go of the toilet seat lid. He wouldn't let go of my legs. I prayed for someone to come in the door and catch him. How long had he been in here? Was he going to assault me?

And as quickly as he had entered the bathroom, he released his grip and left just as quickly. It was such a shock. I used my arms to pull myself back into the stall, pulled my pants back up and bolted out the door looking for my attacker. I spotted a man walking briskly away, black shiny hair, stocky build, the identifiable plaid shirt . . . and wearing an orange store employee apron. I ran to find Gil.

"Gil, this man just attacked me in the bathroom and I think he works here. He dragged me part way out of the stall onto the floor. I want him arrested!"

The shock had turned to disbelief. Why did this happen to me? Then I began to shake, getting sick to my stomach.

We went to find the manager. A young guy in his early twenties with blond hair who was sitting on a tabletop said, "Yeah, I'm the manager today . . . what's up?"

My face grew hot as I began to tell him what had happened. I watched as his face broke into a grin.

"Well, that's a new one. He really did that?"

Gil was perturbed with him. He was treating it like a joke.

"Is that all you've got to say?" Gil fired back.

"Hey, I'm just saying, that's pretty weird, don't you think?"

I began to feel like the butt of a bad joke. That's when I'd had enough.

"Call the police. Call them right now! Gil, tell him . . ."

Now it was Gil who was acting humiliated. He took my hand and became very stern.

"No, we're not calling the police. Let's just get out of here," and led me out the door. That's when I became angry at three men: my attacker, the manager and my husband. I let a rapist get off free as a bird in 1976 and I didn't want one more abusive man loose to do whatever he pleased. I didn't realize how traumatizing it was until a few months later. No more extra cups of coffee for me. I couldn't think of using a public restroom. Then for a time I wouldn't use one unless I checked it first and Gil stood outside to wait for me. I knew I couldn't do that forever, so I purchased a small jackknife to carry in my purse. I had it open and ready anytime I was in a bathroom stall. I wasn't afraid to cut someone and make them bleed for reaching underneath my door. At least there'd be DNA left at the scene.

Chapter 54

EMERGENCY TRAUMA TIME

After traveling to Flint, Michigan for two grueling days of nursing state boards, all the preparation would soon be over. Four of us met at a motel near the testing facility and settled in with books and study notes packed in our well-worn backpacks. After day one with the testing only half over, several people had accepted defeat and gone home. Others went back to their motel rooms and began to try and cram for the next day. I decided to go to the movies and out for Chinese food. I figured if I didn't know it by then, I never would. My friends ended up joining me and it turned into a fun, relaxing evening. At the end of day two, we all knew the test scores would decide our fate and that we would be waiting a month or two before learning the results. Eventually, all four of us would finally be able to celebrate.

I started my new nursing position on the afternoon shift in the emergency trauma center of an inner city hospital which I nicknamed, "the blood and guts place." We got every type of case imaginable. The doctors there were phenomenal, hard working and devoted. The residents in training were really talented and it was easy to tell who would probably remain in the emergency field. However, there's generally one that you wish would change.

"Hey, so what is it with him? He's been grumpy and moody for two weeks. I'm so sick of him being an ass. What should we do?"

Everyone made a suggestion and we all settled on one which required taking up a collection. We circled the staff with everyone pitching in what money they could and handed it over to one of the resident physicians in charge of the collection.

"I'll take it from here," he chuckled. "We're getting him a hooker."

Then there was a game that was a version of The Price Is Right. When a drunk was brought in that had refused to let a policeman administer a breathalyzer test, his blood was drawn and the alcohol level was obtained for the police. Before the test result was in, we'd take a guess at the number and kick in a dollar. Whoever was the closest without going over won the pot. I got pretty good at it just by smelling their breath. It was a simple diversion from what was often a very stressful job.

One summer night I was privileged to witness a near-miracle. A male teenager stumbled in through the doors holding up a young man with him whose shirt was saturated with blood. He'd been stabbed in the chest. We got him on a gurney and immediately started two intravenous lines. Losing so much fluid so fast can be deadly and he would quickly need blood. The primary physician saw him and frowned as the patient began having breathing problems.

The doctor talked about "cracking his chest," which entailed opening up the chest and spreading the ribs. A call was made to the surgical resident who was sleeping upstairs. Within thirty seconds Rex was fully awake standing over the boy, quickly opening up his chest, feeling inside. The knife had punctured his heart and Rex was feeling for the hole. Just then, his scrub pants began to fall down exposing a large portion of his bare buttocks.

"Beth, grab Rex's pants – they're falling off."

"No way I'm touching them when he's got this guy's heart in his hand."

Seconds later, Rex had his finger in the heart like a hole in the dike, and we were off, driving the gurney down the hallway to the elevator and up to a surgical suite with breakneck speed. There was blood everywhere – a trail of it down the entire hall and into the elevator. We never got Rex's pants up where they belonged. It wasn't important. Minutes later we got a call from the O.R. Rex stitched up his heart and he was critical but stable. There were tears in our eyes. Rex was incredible and we were all so proud of him. Three weeks later, that boy walked out the doors of our hospital. I will never forget it as long as I live and I still get choked up talking about it.

Chapter 55

DRIFTING ON DIFFERENT SHIFTS

It never concerned me that Gil and I wouldn't be able to handle the afternoon shift. Since we had talked about him going on afternoons if that was the shift I had to take, I thought it was settled. It wasn't.

"Gil, when are you putting in for afternoons? I miss us not being together more."

"Well, I've decided to stay on days."

"But I thought we already agreed that we would take the same shift. We talked about this before. I didn't have a choice and you said that with your seniority, you could work any shift you choose. What happened to that?"

"I decided I like the day shift better, so I'm staying on days."

I felt hurt and stymied. It seemed important enough to talk about two years earlier. With both of our track records in marriage, I wanted this one to last and working different shifts seemed to be asking for discord. I'd be on my way to work at 1:30 p.m.; he was on his way home about 3 p.m. He'd go to bed about 10 p.m.; I wouldn't get home until after 12:30 a.m. and would be too wound up to sleep until about 2 a.m. He'd get up at 5:00 a.m. So, we only ate meals together on my days off and I was scheduled to work every other weekend. There were nurses with fifteen years in that couldn't get on days, so I knew my chances were next to nothing to be able to transfer.

He got involved in a jewelry making class in the evenings. I went to the gym many mornings. One morning in when we were both home, he made an announcement.

"I'm tired of this house and the neighborhood. There's nothing for us here. Let's sell the house and move. I want to move to Florida when I retire and you said you didn't want to move again unless it was on or near the water, so let's go look at houses."

It was 1994 and that would make it three moves for me in six years. It was August when we went to see a house on Elizabeth Lake, the opposite end of where Greg and I had lived. The house had been occupied by renters for seven years and was in pretty rough shape. Ours wasn't sold yet, but we had interested buyers. Another couple was making an offer on the same home as we were. It was their intention to have the house torn down and build a new place. Their house hadn't sold yet either. It turned into a race to the finish; ours sold first and our deal went through. Gil already had his mental wrecking ball ready before we even had the closing.

Chapter 56

LAKEFRONT MOVE BUT NO BOAT

We closed on our lakefront home in September of 1994. I loved the thought of being back on the water—the smell of it, the waves lapping the shore—it was all so comfortable. It made me feel like I was living at a vacation spot. I grew up on this lake and it suited me. Since we were very careful with our money and had even paid cash for Gil's new truck, it seemed to make sense to talk about looking for a boat but Gil wouldn't have it.

"No, we're not getting a boat until this house is finished."

"Finished? Gil, there's a ton of work here. Let's at least get a boat we can relax on after a hard day's work on this place."

"No, I say the house comes first."

Then the sledge hammering began on the walls of one of the bedrooms upstairs. It had truly been a neglected house, but a solid one. That fall, I took my sax out onto the upper deck and began playing, listening to the sound echoing back to me from across the water. I played the song, "New York, New York" and before I was finished Canadian geese began landing all over the yard. It was an unbelievable sight. A couple more choruses and there were at least eighty between the lakeshore and the house. One of the neighbors was not amused. I thought it was hilarious until I walked down to the lake the next morning. There wasn't a place I could find to step without meeting up with a pile of goose poop.

We decided to have some plans drawn up and check the feasibility of overhauling the house and garage. When toying with the idea of finishing off each level and treating them like separate entities, it seemed to open up more possibilities. Gil and I both loved to travel. Maybe we could find someone trustworthy to live downstairs and keep an eye on the house while we disappeared to parts unknown. The kitchen downstairs was dark; the wood cupboards and even the scant amount of natural light made it somewhat dreary. Coupling that with the low ceilings, it seemed a bit claustrophobic. We would definitely have to live upstairs, no matter what.

Chapter 57

DON'T TOUCH

Soon the fall weather slid into winter; immediately our backyard view took on the appearance of the frozen tundra. Suddenly, Florida was sounding very good. Gil wanted to visit with his son and my parents had invited us to come down and stay for a bit. They were on opposite sides of the state but we were willing to drive across to see everyone. I decided to have some sexy pictures taken by a local glamour photographer and give them to Gil for Valentine's Day, the same week we'd be vacationing in Florida.

The photo shoot was great fun. The photographer was female, so dressing scantily and mostly in feather boas wasn't too unnerving. She seemed surprised at a really important question I asked.

"Would you take some pictures of me with my sax?"

"Sax as in saxophone? Why would you want to do that?"

"Because I love playing sax and I have fantasies about playing on stage wearing a low cut short black dress and spike heels with beads of perspiration on my cleavage."

"Well . . . okay then, let's shoot it."

We settled on taking the picture with me wearing a teddy and turned out to be the best, most sensual picture in whole bunch. I could hardly wait to see if Gil liked it. I ordered several other provocative pictures staged in different colored backgrounds, outfits and poses, and placed them all into a small photo album, tucking it away for Valentine's Day.

Burnout while working in an emergency trauma center is pretty common and I was so ready for a break from it. After working ten-hour shifts for four days running, I came home pretty exhausted one night. I crawled into bed about one o'clock in the morning and put my arm over Gil's waist and began to nuzzle closely to him. I assumed he was asleep until I heard him.

"Don't touch me."

"What? What did you say, Hun?" I thought maybe he was dreaming. I wasn't sure I had understood him.

"I said . . . don't touch me."

"Why? What's wrong?"

"I don't know."

I rolled away from him over to the other side of the bed, lying there in disbelief. It was confusing. It didn't make sense to me. We hadn't even had a spat, let alone any fight. I didn't sleep the rest of the night. Three days later, he moved out of the bedroom, clothes and all.

"Gil, are you having an affair? Is there someone else? Just tell me if there is . . . I need to know."

"No, I'm not having an affair and there's no one else."

"Then why? Why can't I touch you anymore? Why won't you sleep in the same bed with me? I'm not a pig, I'm not disgusting. What's happened? What changed?"

There was no reply, no answer. Our vacation to Florida was the following week and I was now dreading it. He was very quiet driving to the airport and on the flight.

We arrived at my folks' condo a little over an hour after landing at West Palm Beach International Airport. Mom and I took a walk down to the clubhouse on the water. There was a warm breeze blowing down the Intracoastal and the water smelled heavenly. I began staring into space. I knew Mom's radar would be working.

"What's going on with you two?"

"Mom, I really don't know. I don't think Gil wants to be with me anymore. He's rejecting me and I don't know why. He moved out of our bedroom. He won't tell me what's wrong. I feel like he's totally pushed me away." Tears began to drip off my face onto the warm concrete.

She had a look of deepened concern on her face.

"I thought he was really the one for you. You two seemed so happy."

"I thought we were too. This has really knocked the wind out of me."

We continued going through the motions of the semblance of a couple. On Valentine's Day, I gave Gil his gift, the photo album wrapped in colorful paper. It seemed so lackluster now. He opened it, thumbed quickly through the pictures and handed it back to me.

"That's nice."

That was all. Next was the trip across the state to see his son, his son's wife, and their baby daughter. I tried keeping up a good face, but it was very difficult. Somehow, I knew this would be our last vacation together and it broke my heart.

Chapter 58

SANDY THE PSYCHOLOGIST

I was really distraught when we returned from Florida in February, 1995. I thought that if I was able to run the recent turn of events by a counselor it might help me deal with it. I sought out someone I could trust and Sandy was that person. Our first three weeks delved strictly into the past. I was told that it was important to go back in time and work our way through to the present. We talked about my family life growing up and my relationship with my parents. Then it progressed to my first love and how it felt to get a Dear Jane letter ending things. Next were discussions about my self-loathing for not getting on that plane back in 1969 and how long I continued to kick myself for not fulfilling my dream with Holiday on Ice. We turned to my first marriage fraught with intimidation and domination which choked out the love I had to give. I told her about dreams of being locked in dark places like a coffin that I didn't belong in and a closet where I couldn't seem to breathe, begging to be released.

When the conversation reached into the early 80's and Greg, nicknamed "the bad man" I had married, the memories of lying in the chilly water in a bathtub for eighteen hours of my life, not knowing if I would live or die – it all came creeping back and settled, surrounding me like a thick foreboding black smoke. It was hard to contain myself; I tried not to weep, but the hurt and sadness was overwhelming. All this and we hadn't even gotten to the Gil issue. Sandy and I sat looking at each other. I expected questions and instead I got this revelation from her.

"Beth, I think that you've suffered from post-traumatic stress disorder over this. It's common when you've come close to losing your life. I'm sure it's been difficult to accept that someone you professed to love would not only try to hurt you, but possibly try to kill you."

I think that's partly why I remained alone those years after it happened. Who could I trust? How would I ever be able to believe in someone with my heart and my feelings in the balance? Was I willing to have someone take me from my single life of financial independence to leaving me financially ruined again?

And then when I wasn't the least bit looking for anyone, I met this wonderful man named Gil. Here and now, eight years after we met, our relationship was heading into the toilet. I wanted to try couples counseling to get to the bottom of it. Sandy said it required both the husband and wife to be referred for it and Gil would need to be evaluated. He wouldn't agree to see Sandy with me, but said he would "see someone" if he could pick the person. In the meantime, I got a call from an apartment complex close to home where I had filled out an application. There was a first floor a unit that was going to be available in a week or so. It had been torture for me to stay at the house living like a detached roommate. I told the apartment manager that I'd be there to sign the lease my next day off from work.

I didn't want be the one to have to move. But, with the house torn up because the renovation was in progress and all of Gil's tools were there, my moving made the most sense. It was May when Gil helped me move into the one bedroom apartment. I chose a complex within a mile of our home, hoping that if reconciliation was a possibility, the closer in proximity the better. The only things I took with me that I cared about were my piano and my sax. The ground floor apartment had a door wall which made the piano move much easier. My heart ached as the last box was carried in and he pulled his truck out of the parking lot, making a left hand turn onto Cass Elizabeth Lake Road that led back to the house . . . our house. I was alone once again with my forty-fifth birthday rapidly approaching.

Chapter 59

ALONE WITH A PIANO IN TOW

Here I sat surrounded by packing boxes once again and with my two old friends, my 1918 Wheelock five foot grand piano and the alto sax. I didn't have the heart to unpack, so I just played my piano. It kept me in my own little comfort zone. For hours I would sit playing somber tunes about love and love lost until my shoulders ached. The love of playing my sax had vanished. In years past, I'd always had music in my head, sometimes catchy little tunes, a new pop song from the radio or even elevator music. But when the music stopped being there as my comfort and my friend, that was the sign something was very wrong. There was no music or joy left in me.

Apartment living didn't suit me well with some noisy neighbors, and disrespectful, insolent kids hanging out of the second story windows or running up and down the stairs at all hours, sometimes having raw egg fights in the hallways absent of any parental direction. I hoped this would not be a long stay.

In the meantime, Gil said he'd choose a psychologist within the same practice as Sandy which I hoped would expedite things. I continued seeing Sandy weekly for sanity's sake. I signed a form giving her permission to discuss me with his therapist. My shifts at the hospital proved to be more tiring and sleepless nights weren't helping either. I tried to continue my three times a week workouts at Bally's Gym. Then one morning I walked out to my car and there was a note on my windshield held by the wiper blade. It was from Gil.

"Could we meet for breakfast? Please let me know."

My appointment with Sandy was the following day. I wanted some input from her.

"Do you want to see him? It's been some time now. Maybe he's ready to talk. You've been waiting for this."

Since I was the one who wanted answers, I was anxious to have some face-to-face conversation. We talked briefly on the phone and agreed on Saturday morning. We both loved going out for breakfast and had our old standby restaurants where we generally spent lazy Saturday or Sunday mornings sipping coffee and downing a breakfast special. The one on the corner of M-59 and Elizabeth Lake Road was where we chose to meet.

I was anxious driving to the restaurant. Was this a good sign or a bad sign? Would he want to reconcile or would he want to divorce? Anxiety turned to disappointment as I approached the table. The Gil I knew was fastidious about his looks, especially his hair and his clothing. He was sitting in a booth wearing a white undershirt with a hole in the front and his hair looked greasy. I had seen him make more effort to work out in the yard all day. I wondered what that was all about. After weeks, he had very little to say and I left terribly disappointed. There was no warm hug or affection of any kind and my frustration was peaking. This did not go well.

My next visit to Sandy, I expressed my disappointment. She told me Gil had been in to see another therapist and they would be meeting that week to discuss us and whether they could recommend joint marriage counseling. I asked that she call me as soon as possible. I got my answer a week later.

"As I mentioned before, Beth, it was important that both of you meet separately with a counselor and we in turn would discuss whether marriage counseling seemed viable for you both. After talking over the matters at hand, and in order to have it even be considered, there had to be two willing parties. I'm sorry to say that at this point we only have one."

My heart sank and I left her office. I guess this was just a more elaborate way of saying it was over. In August, I filed for divorce.

A few weeks later Gil left a message on my answering machine that I had quite a lot of mail over at the house and I could come by and pick it up. It seemed surreal to have to knock on my own back door. Gil opened the door to let me in, looking expressionless. There was mail strewn all over the countertop in the lower level.

"Geez, that's quite a stack of mail."

"I didn't know you were filing for divorce. You didn't have to. We could stay married in name and both live here, just on different levels."

"It's just not enough for me, Gil. I told you after we first met that in order to get married again I wanted someone to love that would love me back. If you can't do that, then I can't be here.

You still haven't told me what happened and why . . . why did this end so suddenly? I do not understand this and I need to understand, don't you see that? It's tearing me up inside."

"I can't picture myself ever having to push you around in a wheelchair."

"A wheelchair?"

"Yeah."

"Well, you know something Gil, you could get hit by a truck tomorrow and end up in a wheelchair and I would still love you. How about this? How about if my health ever gets bad enough that you might actually have to do something to help me . . . how about if I agree to off myself and put it in writing . . . would that be enough for you?"

"No."

I grabbed my mail off the counter and walked out of the house. He couldn't have hurt me any worse if he'd shoved a knife in my chest. I drove a short distance down the road until I couldn't see through the tears and pulled off onto the shoulder.

I will never forget that day.

Chapter 60

SPARKLING EYES AND COWBOY BOOTS

The house on the water was the center of attention in Gil's and my divorce, but not bickering—just the opposite. He said he didn't want to stay there and would let me buy him out. I couldn't afford the house payment on my nurse's wages, even though I would have loved to remain on the water. He had enough of the house torn apart that I didn't know whether a new mortgage was even attainable. My thoughts were that we both shouldn't have to leave such a good investment behind. I would do what I could so he could keep it even if I had to delay getting my portion of the money out of the house. As it turned out he was able to get a new mortgage and I met him at his closing to sign off on the house. Upon leaving the house earlier that year, I took my late grandmother's silverware with me. It was given to me when she died and I loved her dearly. Knowing how men are about "kitchen things" I assumed Gil had not replaced it, so I bought him a new set of silverware and gave it to him as a housewarming gift in the bank parking lot after the closing. I guess that was my way of closure to the house on the lake. Little did I know then that the closure I needed with Gil was so out of reach.

It was a blustery, winter evening one Friday when I got off work at the hospital. At twelve- thirty in the morning I wasn't the least bit tired. It had been a really, really busy night in the emergency room. It was getting to me coming home to a lonely one bedroom apartment; this wasn't a place I could call "home." I changed into some jeans and drove to a local bar and grill. After deciding to go in, I grabbed twenty dollars in small bills out of my wallet and walked to the trunk of my car to stash my purse. Just then, a fierce gust of wind pulled the trunk lid from my hand and nearly blew me over. My reflex was to grab the lid with both hands and suddenly the money from my hand was swirling in the wind flying off to parts unknown. I wondered if it was an omen – should I just give up, drive back home and call it a night? No, I rationalized. I was there and I was going to stay. I rummaged around the parking lot retrieving thirteen dollars of my money and headed for the front door. It was amazing I found any of it. The jukebox blared from the corner of the bar, the lights were low, and I was comfortable even being surrounded by people I didn't know.

That's when I met Craig. He was slightly taller than I, had a great head of hair, a good physique and sparkling eyes that seemed to dance. I told him about the parking lot experience I just encountered and he guffawed – what a fantastic laugh he had. We talked for awhile and then danced, feeding one quarter after another into the jukebox. He had on tasteful cowboy boots, a long sleeved red shirt and jeans. Needless to say, he was very cute and I liked the sound of his voice.

"I live in the apartments across the street," he said. "What about you?"

"Well, I'm in an apartment about two miles from here, but it's only temporary . . . actually I'm looking for a house to buy. My work's in medicine as a registered nurse. What kind of work do you do? "

"I sell cars at a dealership near here – Fords mostly."

I had never dated a car salesman, so this would be a first. We exchanged a lot of information in the coming months. After high school he ended up in the military and was sent to Viet Nam, as so many young men were in the sixties, he'd been married once and it ended in divorce after his wife had been unfaithful while he was overseas, had one sister, and loved to duck hunt. His apartment was right on Cass Lake and he had a ski boat. We began spending time together on a regular basis. I thought he was smart and sexy. All the while, I was still feeling like an emotional train wreck; Gil's rejection continued to weigh me down like an anchor.

Chapter 61

NEW DIGS

In mid-winter, my realtor and I were still trying to find "the right place" for me. I was ready to tackle a house that needed work. One day while driving by a house on Scott Lake Road, I found it. I had admired the property through the years because of the beautiful sedum growing next to the driveway that led up the incline to the older ranch home. In the fall, the sedum was a gorgeous deep pink-purple color, each plant at least a foot and a half in width and I marveled at how inviting it made the home look. I had never noticed a for sale sign before that day. Excited, I called Patty, my realtor.

"Patty, I think I've found it – it's a house in Waterford and I want to see it as soon as I can. "

"Well, that's great! Give me the address and I'll check to see who the listing agent is and if it's still available."

The next day we were trudging through immense snowdrifts which encircled the house and made our way to the front door.

"Beth, the house has been vacant for at least six months. The lot is nearly an acre and most of those trees in the back yard are fruit trees."

Once we were inside, I was impressed at the workmanship of the cove ceilings and plaster walls. It reminded me of the first home my parents built. There was a beautiful fireplace in both the living room and the family room in the basement. Carpeting covered all the bedroom floors except for the master bedroom which I thought was curious. Several months later I would find out why. There were remnants of another family's life in every room, along with artificial flowers mounted on the walls and in vases. The owners were an elderly couple and the wife had died, leaving her husband behind. He had his yard with the fruit trees to tend to, but being in his eighties, the upkeep of the property which was about an acre must have been overwhelming. The front door had a screen on it with the letters "AB" customized in the center and the same two letters were on the garage door. My nine year old nephew would later tell his mother he knew exactly which house was mine because the "AB" stood for "Aunt Beth."

After negotiating price and terms with the surviving children, the house was mine. There were tears at the closing and learning their father had died, I promised them I would take good care of the house, Arnold's house. The roof shingles desperately needed replacing. A leak had caused some significant damage in one wall but I didn't mind. The original dining room, a small space off the living room would house my piano. The well wasn't working. The basement leaked. However, the view out the back door wall was beautiful and the lot was one-hundred fifty feet wide and three-hundred thirty-five feet deep but it seemed to go back a half a mile. I even inherited a twenty-three year old Wheel Horse tractor.

The move took place in March of 1996 and I was very happy to say goodbye to apartment living. As the moving van began to empty, I finally felt that this would truly be home again for me. Then odd things began to happen and I wondered if trouble had followed me.

As I started arranging the furniture I made a strange discovery. I'd plug in a lamp and the light bulb would explode, leaving me in the dark. Another lamp and another blown bulb; it was crazy. I began checking the fuse boxes in the basement. Was there a power surge problem? I began relying on nightlights so I wouldn't stumble into a wall during the night. I bought all new light bulbs but they continued to pop leaving tiny pieces of glass everywhere. Then lights that were turned off would suddenly come on in the middle of the night, especially in the guest room. An electrician named Ron who was an old friend and former neighbor came over and gave me an estimate on a new breaker box to consolidate the two fuse boxes in the basement. He would change the service the following day.

Then I met a new neighbor named Tom who told me an interesting story about the former owner of my house. Tom had been the one who used the tractor to cut Arnold's lawn for him.

"Yeah, it was really a shame about Arnold. I never saw it coming."

"What coming?"

"You know, how his life ended."

"What do you mean? What happened to him?"

"Oh, I figured you already knew about it. He got pretty depressed when his wife died. He owned some horses and then his favorite horse died. He left a note and took a shotgun and blew himself away right in the bedroom. Are you staying in the back bedroom? That's where it happened."

"Yes, in the room with no carpeting. I guess now that makes sense. I know I'll sound like some kook to you, but there's been something funny happening in that house with the lights and exploding light bulbs. I even had a new electrical service installed, but the lights are still going on and off by themselves. What do you make of that?"

"Oh . . . that Arnold, he must have stuck around."

That was pretty unnerving. A few nights later, my friend, Kip from beauty college came by and the lights suddenly began to flicker. I decided to hit it head on – this needed to stop.

"Arnold, you'll have to cut this out! I won't have you scaring my friends, so stop it!"

My friend looked at me in disbelief. I was bellowing at Arnold, poor dead Arnold. It seemed like a cold thing to do, but the lights flickering and the bulb bursting stopped and it never happened again. I grew fond of Arnold's house and wished I had met him. In his memory, I left the front screen door in place with "AB" on it, just as it should be.

Chapter 62

BREAKING THE BOAT

Once things were more settled, I began one project after another on the house, the yard, and the garage. One day while I was in the garage, a spring from the garage door suddenly broke loose and sailed like a missile past me and lodged itself in the back wall. It was so close to hitting me I felt the breeze on my face. I had no idea those springs could be so treacherous. Three or four inches different from where I was standing and it could have killed me. I ended up having to replace the garage door and of course, the springs. In a matter of months the roof shingles were replaced by a friend I'd met in a restaurant who was in the roofing business. Tom H. saw me looking through pictures I'd taken of the house and a conversation ensued which led to a great and real friendship. In the months to follow, I had demolished the wall in the main bathroom tub enclosure, installed new green board and replaced the ceramic tile, repaired the living room wall (also a victim of the water leak) and lifted twenty-two feet by three feet of basement tile up one by one with a hair dryer and a putty knife. That was to prepare for a company to come in and use an air hammer on the floor to break it up and lay a new drainage system because of water leaking into the basement. The tile was in nice shape and I was unable to match it, so it was important to retain the ones I had to re-lay. Then, I painted the entire main floor of the house. The limestone half-wall window box across the front of the house seemed to be a contributing factor to the basement water problem. I knew it should be torn off but finding someone to hire that would do it was another matter. Being impatient, I took two days off work, borrowed Dad's sledge hammer, decimated the wall and loaded a truck with the chunks of stone.

All in all, it proved very therapeutic to have a house to work on. I drew my own sense of accomplishment from each task I finished and it kept me from being lonely.

Craig began coming around the house after my move and we continued to see one another. He worked long hours as car salespeople do, so our time spent together was limited. Once spring turned to summer, we had something very special in common – the love of the lake. His boat was an older one, but in very nice shape and was perfect for waterskiing. He had launched it in Cass Lake and was excited to get out on the water as often as he could. However the third week in June would prove to be a challenge for me. He called about getting together over the weekend.

"Would you like to come over and go out on the boat Sunday? There's somebody I want you to meet."

"Who's that, Craig?"

"My son – I don't see him much and he's agreed to come over this weekend."

"Gee, you never mentioned you had a son. Sure, I'd like to meet him."

When I arrived at his apartment, I found them down at the boat ready to go. His son was cordial and appeared to be in his early twenties with a lanky build. We pulled out from shore with water skis, tow ropes, and beach towels and a cooler on hand. The sun was shining brightly and it looked like a great day to be on the water. But once out taking a ride, it was clear that the boat traffic was overwhelming. On one end of the lake there was a deep circular area that attracted skiers, similar to a lagoon.

"Hey, let's head over there, Beth."

"Looks like other people had the same idea, Craig. This just isn't going to be a good day to ski."

"Oh, it'll be fine. You can pull me."

"I don't really want to drive, Craig. There's too much traffic."

Craig asked his son to drive, but he declined. Then Craig insisted I drive the boat, becoming pretty miffed with me. If we had been alone, the answer would have remained a resounding "no," but with Craig's son with us, it was uncomfortable. To keep the peace and against better judgment, I reluctantly got behind the wheel of the boat. I was a skilled boater having driven for over twenty years pulling skiers, and that's what made me wary. Too much boat traffic makes for lousy skiing, too. Craig grabbed his slalom ski and dove off the boat with the tow rope handle in his hand.

We traveled all the way around the lagoon area until we reached the opening to head out into the large part of the lake. The opening was cluttered with dead tree branches on the left and very swiftly, a sailboat began to cut across the opening directly in front of us. I had no choice but to power down the boat, as sailboats have the right of way. As Craig sunk slowly down into the water he began yelling.

"What the hell happened? Why'd you stop?"

I motioned to the sailboat which was now directly in our path. He was irritated.

"Head back around there again then!" he snapped.

As we began to accelerate to make the wide circle once more and were halfway around, the boat suddenly lost power and quickly coasted to a stop. Once again, Craig sunk into the water when the tow rope went limp.

"Damn it! What's wrong now? There's nothing else in front of you, is there?"

"I didn't do anything, Craig. It just lost power."

He swam furiously toward the boat. "Give me my mask!"

His son handed him the diving mask and before he finish saying, "Dad, she really didn't do anyth...," Craig was already under water inspecting the boat. His head reappeared and he threw the mask into the boat.

"Do you know what you've done? You broke the goddamn prop shaft! What the hell were you thinking? You probably did it when you stopped the boat back there. What did you do, slam the boat on the bottom of the lake? This is just great."

"Craig, we drove half way around again before the boat stopped. Why is it all my fault?"

"Because it is . . . are you stupid? Now, how do you think we're going to get back to shore, just tell me that?"

The sound was carrying across the water. There was a couple sitting on a pontoon boat not too far away from us. The man was standing with his hands on his hips and called to Craig.

"Hey, do you need a tow in?"

"We sure do, thanks to her."

I was bewildered and embarrassed. His son stayed silent. The man with the pontoon boat threw Craig a rope.

"Just tie it on the front. We'll get you back home."

As we were being towed, Craig got heated once more. He was pacing in the boat and then started in on me again then he turned to the man towing us.

"You know, we wouldn't be in this mess if she hadn't wrecked my boat. I told her where to drive. I didn't think I needed to tell her how to drive. She wouldn't have gotten it anyway."

It wasn't enough that I felt bad that this had to happen while I was driving but it had reached humiliation. It was an older boat. Maybe it had been cracked for a year and had to give way while I was behind the wheel. I didn't know and neither did he, but he just wouldn't let up. Then came his last stinging sentence.

"Why don't you just get out of my sight . . . you make me sick. There's nothing like putting the screws to the Fourth of July weekend for me."

Yes, the Fourth was only days away and I had heard enough and had enough. With that, I dove off the side of the boat and began the swim for shore, heavy boat traffic and all—anything to make him stop. Craig motioned to the man to tow the boat to the marina directly across the bay from Craig's apartment so the man towed him directly to it. I considered getting into my car soaking wet and driving home and not looking back, leaving them to haul the skis and other equipment back to the apartment by themselves. But, when I reached shore, I felt some perverted sense of duty and decided to stick it out. I drove over to the marina to help just as the boat was being pulled out of the water, with Craig giving the mechanics his version of my recklessness. Craig began swearing at me and stormed onto the boat and began throwing the equipment off. One of the mechanics took my arm and said, "Listen, don't let him blame you for this—it's not your fault, got it? Lots of things can cause this. If this is your boyfriend, he's an ass."

I quietly asked Craig when he settled down if he wanted me to take the skis and cooler back in the car and offered to drive him and his son back to the apartment and I did. Once the car was unloaded and his son headed toward the apartment with the cooler and life jackets, Craig looked at me and said, "Thanks for nothing!" and walked at a hurried pace to the apartment door carrying his ski, tow rope, and towels.

I stopped by my parents' house on the way home to change my clothes and explained what happened to Dad. It was his thoughtful words that made me feel better.

"Now you know you've driven boats long enough to know what to do. If you had to stop for a sailboat, then you had to.

You're anything but reckless. Did <u>you</u> wreck his boat? I really doubt it. Don't second guess anything just because he's acting like a jerk."

On Monday afternoon, July 1st, I called the marina to see if I could talk to the mechanic.

"Listen, I was with the boat owner yesterday when the boat was towed in. It would mean so much to him if it could be repaired by the Fourth. What are the chances?"

"Depends on how quickly we can get the parts."

"I'll pay you $300 over the repair expense to have it fixed before the Fourth of July. Here's my name and number and call me when you know and I'll pay you. Thanks."

Tuesday, I got an unexpected phone call. It added insult to injury.

"Who in the hell do you think you are calling and sticking your nose in my business about <u>my</u> boat?"

"Craig, I was just trying to help."

"Oh, you've already 'helped' enough already. Go to hell."

The boat was repaired and in the water in time for Craig and his out-of-town family members to enjoy. I spent my birthday, July 3rd alone and July 4th with my family. Guess that's the way it was meant to be.

Chapter 63

JAIL WORK AND JEALOUSY

In the fall of 1996, I received a visit from Craig. He brought my belated birthday present with him and a request that we try again. It was difficult to give him a second chance. His behavior hadn't earned it. In the midst of my summer I had also heard from Gil. His reason for calling was quite different.

"Beth, I just got back from having my hair cut and this girl butchered it. Do you think you can fix it? I always liked the way you cut my hair. Do you think we can work something out? I can either pay you or we can barter—maybe there's something around your house that I can do for you. Can I come over?"

"Yes, make it about an hour. I'm in the middle of something."

As I brushed the dirt from my overalls, I thought back – I had cut Gil's hair for about seven years and I had been happy to do it. Was the only reason he wanted to come over because of his hair? Was he at all interested in seeing me for me? I had mixed feelings but figured that if it did nothing but open the conversation to the reason for our breakup – the reason our marriage truly ended – it would be worth it. He just wasn't leveling with me and I knew it. I needed the whole truth because only imagining was much more painful. Yes, I'm a woman who needed that thing—that "closure" that men hate to hear about. He arrived an hour later.

"So this is the place you bought. Do you like it here?"

"It's nothing like living on the lake, but it is my home for now."

Yes, Gil was right. The girl that cut his hair could have used an egg beater and done a better job. There were large gouges in the crown and on one side of his head.

"Gil, I'm going to have to take more off to even it out. You know your hair grows fast. It'll be back at the length you like within two or three weeks."

"Okay, do it."

I had hoped I was laying the groundwork for some honesty with his next visit. I let him pay me. It was a bargain for him but I knew it could turn out to mean much more to me.

Work in the emergency room was changing. Our ten-hour shifts four days a week were going to be done away with. The afternoon 2 pm to 12 midnight shift I was on was soon to disappear leaving days and midnights. I only had five years seniority and knew I would have to go to the midnight shift. I had never been able to sleep during the day – it made midnights seem impossible so I began looking for something else.

The Oakland County complex was close by and the benefits were good. I took their nursing exam on my day off and received a phone call a few weeks later. I was given a tour of my new workplace – the Oakland County Jail with a starting date in February of 1997 on the afternoon shift. It was a very tough assignment. Nurses there covered the entire jail, both male and female prisoners. Pedophiles were the most orderly and cooperative prisoners. Many of the women incarcerated were hardened and crude. Male cells with ten to fourteen inmates each were the most lewd because of their instantly available audience for acting out. Prisoners with full blown Aids were in private cells and the amount of medications they took daily was staggering. Killers were scary. With all of the prisoners, you were taught to hold the medicine cup just so . . . otherwise you may be grabbed and pulled at the wrist and have your face slammed into the iron bars. In the more dangerous areas, a deputy would be assigned to accompany the nurses.

The jail had an unusually putrid odor, an offensive one permeating the hallways. I was told it was the smell of the wax on the floors. What on earth was in that wax? Because of a shortage of parking spaces, getting to work very early was necessary to get a parking place nearby. There seemed to be mandatory overtime nearly every night and dealing with heavy medication carts and heavier doors made the job taxing. But the coworkers made it worthwhile. They worked hard which I appreciated and there were good supervisors. Occasionally, a deputy or nurse would celebrate a birthday and we'd meet at a local bar for a drink after work. I made a point of inviting Craig to join us and sometimes he would. Since he sold cars, I thought it might lead to some decent business for him and reduce the chance of jealousy coming into play. He had already made some comments about me wearing "sexy scrubs," a statement I considered an oxymoron. I saw nothing sexy about scrubs.

On one of those after work celebrations, I called Craig and he declined. I got out of work that night about 12:30, even though the shift ended at 11:00 pm. I did stop by the bar, had a drink, talked to coworkers and headed home. My phone was ringing as I walked in the door.

"Hi. Did you just get home?'

"Yes, Craig. I'm sorry you didn't join us."

"Well, I've been thinking about you and I want to come over and make love to you."

"You do? Right now? It's 1:30 in the morning."

"I can keep you awake. I'll see you in a few."

Come over he did. And yes, we made love, and everything was wonderful until the morning. Instead of cuddling up and enjoying each other I awoke to accusations and crass comments.

"I know what you're up to, what you've been doing. You're up there at that jail flirting with all the deputies and probably more. So how many have you been seeing up there – two, three, maybe four guys? You might as well tell me because I'll find out sooner or later."

"Craig, I'm not seeing anyone else. That's where I work. You're my boyfriend. We've been through a lot. If I wanted to be with someone else, I wouldn't have let you come over and share my bed, would I?"

"How should I know? Maybe there's a different guy that comes home with you every night. What happened last night? Didn't get lucky?"

"Who do you think you are, talking to me like that? You know, I think it's time for you to leave right now."

I left the room holding my clothes and changed in the bathroom. When I came out, he was dressed and heading toward the front door. I followed him as he stormed out toward his car. As he climbed in and slammed the door, he lowered the window.

"You know something, Beth? I shouldn't be with a woman I can't trust and I don't trust you, not one bit. I shouldn't have to put up with that. I guess we should end things now."

"You know, you're right, Craig, you shouldn't be with me if you don't trust me, because if you can't trust me, I don't know that you'll ever trust any woman. I've never lied to you and have never cheated on you. Yes, you're right to break it off, absolutely right."

He backed up until he was on my circle drive and then sped off onto the highway. It was over, so very over.

Chapter 64

GAVIN DE BECKER WAS MY HERO, OR:
Stalker on a Bike
Switching Cars
In a Black Suit Wearing White Paint

My last words with Craig proved to be the beginning of a harrowing string of episodes that I thought would never end. My initial feeling after the breakup was relief. The memories of the jealousy that had become an integral part of my first marriage lit up like a flare. What a huge red flag it had become. I knew I would not and could not put up with it for the rest of my natural life.

Within a matter of days, Craig began calling the house. Foolishly, I answered the phone and from the conversation that ensued, I knew it was a mistake. I told him again that he was right to break up with me and it was better to leave things as they were, but then he'd call back wanting to argue about it. The phone would ring twenty, thirty, forty times in the evening and late into the night. I was becoming anxious each night and unable to sleep. Then a few days later I raised my garage door to back out to leave for work, and suddenly he was there blocking my path with his car. He began pounding on my car window demanding that I talk to him. It was making me a nervous wreck. By the end of that week I'd become overwrought and called my sister Leesa who empathized with me and shared some worthwhile information.

"Beth, there was this author on Oprah today. His name's Gavin de Becker and he wrote a book called, 'The Gift of Fear.' You need to get that book and read it."

Leesa, a smart young woman, wife and mother was so definitive I knew I should listen. I snuck quietly into my garage, carefully looking for signs of tampered windows and doors and drove to the nearest bookstore and back. I stayed up the entire night reading, and getting my mental ammunition in order.

A quote from his book was very telling. "There's a lesson in real-life stalking cases that young women can benefit from learning: Persistence only proves persistence—it does not prove love. The fact that a romantic pursuer is relentless doesn't mean you are special—it means he is troubled." Then there was an important three-word statement. "Do not negotiate." I learned from this book that my wishes only had to be said to Craig once and no more. I had my chance two days later. Peering out my living room window looking for the hiding places he was using for his car became second nature. Since he was so attuned to my whereabouts, I assumed he was parking across the street in a condominium complex that faced my house and a two-lane highway separated us. Not spotting his vehicle, I jumped into my car, put the garage door up and within seconds he was blocking me in my driveway only in a different car. It hadn't occurred to me that he would "borrow" cars off the used car lot where he worked and pull up in an unfamiliar vehicle. He stormed up to my car and demanded I roll down the window and talk to him. It was my opening for the "final statement" with the window open barely two inches and I rammed through my rehearsed message.

"Craig, listen to me because I'm going to say this only once. We are not going to date each other anymore. I am not interested. It's not up for discussion—I'm done. Please move on because I am, and move your car now."

In spite of his ranting, I rolled up the window and stared straight ahead. He clearly had no intention of letting me out of my driveway. I drove over the grass and down the slope of the yard onto the highway and disappeared as quickly as I could. I wondered if I would now have some peace. It was not to be. The phone continued to ring and ring at all hours ruining any chance of a good night's sleep. Even though the book expressed that personal protection orders were not necessarily the answer, I felt desperate enough to drive to the Oakland County Courthouse and see what it would take to file a PPO if it seemed I had no recourse.

The documents were formal and having to go before a judge about it was almost scary. I didn't want to damage Craig's life. I just needed him to stop his behavior. Sitting in the courthouse corridor, I carefully folded the unfiled papers and pushed them into my purse. It would be my last resort.

That evening there was a terrible thunderstorm. I'd been afraid of storms since my childhood and hated being alone during one. The crash of thunder following that quick flash of light was unnerving. It was pitch-black at nearly two in the morning when a fierce wind began blowing branches into the house while rain pounded on the windows. As the noise became more definitive, I rolled over in bed to see Craig's face there. He was striking the bedroom window with his fists until the first pane of glass cracked. Fearing the next blow would send shards of glass all over the bed, I began to panic. Grabbing the cordless phone and slithering across the floor in the dark, I called the police, and said, "Please come right away—I'm afraid he's going to break in!" I never wanted it to come to this – calling the police on him, but I caved in because of the intensity of all of it.

The police were there within minutes as I stood shaking by the front door in the dark clutching the phone tightly. If he came in through the bedroom window, I was going to run out the front door and into the street if I had to.

"Ma'am, whoever was there is gone now. There's muddy footprints back there but no sign of him."

Lucky him. If they had caught up with him that night, I would have wanted him thrown in jail for scaring me so badly. But the flip side was that I was working at that very jail where he would have been held which could make things very uncomfortable for both of us.

I moved out of my house the next morning after packing a week's supply of uniforms and headed over to my parents' house nearby. I arranged to have my paper stopped and my mail held at the post office. At least I felt safer with others around and was able to sleep through the night. I promised myself that if I had to go back to the house, I would go in and get out in five minutes, rehearsing it in my mind. I would not stop more than twice in a week and never at the same time of day.

The first time I tried, it worked and I was really pleased with myself, actually grinning as I departed unscathed. How can he afford to miss so much work staking out my house? He'll have to get bored sometime doing this for very long. Four days later, I stopped before work to grab some clothes, backing carefully into my garage and closing the door. Five minutes passed quickly. Cautiously glancing about, I pulled out of the garage thinking once again it was mission accomplished. Then out of nowhere, Craig rode up on a bicycle and latched onto my door handle with a death grip.

"You're not leaving, no, not until you talk to me!" he howled. "I'm not letting go!"

That panicky feeling returned and needing to escape I began to drive down the driveway with him balancing on his bike and maintaining a firm grasp on the door handle. As I began to turn right onto Scott Lake Road, he suddenly was swung into oncoming traffic. A car skidded to a stop barely missing him. So this is what it's come to, I thought—I could have gotten him killed. I began sobbing in the car, not looking back.

Days later I realized I wanted to go back and live in my house again. On my next day off work I talked to Tom, my brother about it.

"Do you want me to go talk to him? I will if you think it'll help."

I reluctantly said yes, against the advice in Gavin de Becker's book. He writes, "Some victims think it will help to have a male friend, new boyfriend, or a male family member tell the stalker to stop. Most who try this learn that the stalker takes it as evidence that his love object must be conflicted. Otherwise she'd have told him herself." As a desperate person taking desperate measures, I told myself that my brother Tom would be able to talk to him in a rational manner. I nervously waited to hear something back when Tom stopped to see me.

"Well, he seems like a nice guy, but he's just taking this hard. We talked for about two hours. He promised though, that he'll leave you alone and I think he means it."

Cautiously optimistic, I packed my things and headed home. I missed the comforts of my own place, my piano, and my favorite music playing on the stereo. I also thought I had overstayed my welcome at the folks' house. My first night after moving back, all was calm and it provided relief.

There was a gentle rain most of the next day and I spent the time cleaning, doing laundry, and playing my piano. That evening when the rain stopped, I wandered out into the front yard to check for night crawlers in the grass. I had learned how to catch them as a child and relished not having to get the shovel out and dig for worms. The weather for the weekend would be perfect for fishing. Grabbing an empty coffee can and a flashlight, I began to cross the lawn as if in slow motion, putting one bare foot gently down into the slippery wet grass while carefully picking up the other.

My concentration was broken for a split second when directly ahead of me and behind a large bush was the sight of one bright yellow boot, the same style worn by kids at a bus stop on rainy days. This person was balanced motionless on one foot.

"You come out of there! What are you doing back there?"

Wearing a rain slicker and the yellow boots, the culprit stepped out from behind the bush. It was Craig, looking sheepishly at me. I shined the flashlight directly into his eyes. It hadn't even been twenty-four hours since Tom heard him promise to quit stalking me.

"What are you doing here, Craig? You need to leave."

"Watcha doing? What's the can for?"

I've blown it, I thought. Now I've talked to him again. Bad move.

"It's for night crawlers which I'll have to get some other time. Go home."

As I hurried through the front door, flashes of memories during better times popped into my head. We used to have fun together I thought. Why did it end so badly? I remembered not too long before we had gone on our first shopping spree together. A Crowley's store closed in Birmingham and we found Craig some beautiful sheets for his bed and an incredible black dress suit. He looked terrific in it. It needed minor alterations, but when they were finished, it fit like a glove. I knew that the next special occasion, he'd be wearing it.

Summer was fleeting and I needed to get my window casings repainted. I had done the sanding, but decided to hire an old neighbor of mine named Tim to do the painting. He had his own painting business and had done nice work for me in the past. I trusted Tim with a key to my house and left for the day. Upon my return, his truck was gone and the windows were propped open drying. There were some areas on one casing where the paint was smudged off. That wasn't like Tim—he was fussy about his work. As I entered the house I met an intruder head-on. Craig was standing in my living room wearing his new black suit which was now covered in white paint. Now I knew where the smudges came from.

"What are you doing in here? How dare you break into my house!"

"I didn't break in—I came through the window."

"Yeah, and you've got paint all over your suit to prove it!"

Seeing him standing there with all that wet paint everywhere was more than I could take. I began to cry and mumbled something about getting a can of Goo Gone to try and salvage his suit. I knew it might ruin the material but the paint came right off. My hands shook as I tackled each splotch until they were all gone.

"Now go . . . get out of here! Please go."

Tim returned after Craig was gone. I told him not to leave anything open again. He hadn't known about "my problem" and because of it, he had some touching up to do.

There were other instances. Another guy I had just met and started dating was over visiting when Craig burst through the front door demanding I give him a pair of his shorts that were left at my house. My new date thought he was a crazy person. Then, when my roofer friend, Tom was over helping me hang some paneling in my basement recreation room, Craig snuck down the stairs with a hammer in his hand and demanded to know who he was and what he was doing in my house. I was fearful that he may do something awful with the hammer. It was very tense until I began yelling at him to leave and followed him up the stairs. Tom had left the door unlocked when he went to the garage to trim the paneling with his saw. It was all so surreal.

It took several months before all of the attempts ceased. About a year after it all began, my phone rang one evening. The familiar voice that was once threatening now seemed very subdued as we shared a very brief conversation.

"Hi stranger, this is Craig. Say, listen . . . I called to say hello and to apologize for the way I acted. I know you could have had me thrown in jail. I was just acting crazy and I know it. I'm really sorry."

It was music to my ears. Thank you, Gavin. And yes, you are my hero.

236

Chapter 65

BAD MEMORIES = GOOD MOVE

My time working at the jail had certainly been an education. I always felt though, that there was an undercurrent of danger there and it wasn't wise to let my guard down. One particular evening I met a prisoner that had the persona of Charles Manson both in looks and mannerisms. He was in an isolated cell, and generally prisoners were in that area because they were too dangerous to have with other inmates, or they caused problems. A deputy was assigned to accompany me into the isolation areas. Each afternoon I would have to take "Charlie" his medications and he would be pacing wildly back and forth like a tiger in a cage. My job was to make sure he had a cup of water with which to take his meds, and then I'd have to ask him to open his mouth and check that the pills had been swallowed. Inmates got very good at "cheeking" their pills and would save them to trade later for something else. It was an impossible part of the job. With Charlie, I assumed he needed his meds more for psych issues. He'd gotten rather belligerent in recent days and would have to be asked several times to get his water. The day before, his behavior had gotten more bizarre when I came to his cell. He stared at me as if he wanted to see me dead, never stopping his glare while he backed up to his toilet. Then he dipped his water cup into the unflushed toilet and washed down his pills with it in two gulps. It was disgusting. I dreaded returning to his cell the next day. The deputy with me was glancing around as I got another dose of the "I want you dead" look. Once again, with his eyes locked on me, he backed up to the unflushed toilet dipped his cup in, and suddenly decided his pills were not on the agenda. Instead, he showered me with his urine and feces, and some of it splashed onto the deputy's freshly cleaned and pressed uniform pants. I was stunned. The runoff began to drip down from my hair onto my face, and the front of my uniform was spattered with it in a degrading fashion. The deputy was fuming mad, calling for assistance on the radio and within seconds deputies were literally jumping over me to get to his cell. That was the very moment I decided the jail could do without me and I could do without it. I gave two week's notice the following day – no regrets.

I had a few brief relationships with men after Craig. John told me of his divorce and said he was looking for love and companionship. He took me on his boat several times, to a family get-together, and even to a party at his ex-brother-in-law's house. We began looking at homes weekend after weekend while his house was on the market. Then the lie surfaced when his wife's psychiatrist wanted him present at one of her sessions. There had never been a divorce, merely a "separation." Next was a charming slightly younger man named Bill whose company I really enjoyed, but he had an inheritance coming and was not terribly motivated to get a job. We visited a lot of garage sales together, though. Art was a really nice guy and had a Persian cat that upchucked fur balls everywhere. When he became more interested in his incessant e-mails than verbally finishing a sentence with me, it was time to move on.

The traffic in front of my home backed up daily because of the railroad tracks that ran all the way to General Motors. I constantly had to pick up trash from my yard as litterbugs heaved it out of their car windows. The acre of land I sat on was higher maintenance than I expected. I was getting fed up with all of it, so one day in February of 1998 I decided to leave the memories behind and I put my house up for sale. It would be a good move for me.

Chapter 66

CONDO HEAVEN

It took less than two weeks before I had an offer on my Scott Lake Road house. I still found myself suddenly awakening, and nervously staring out my bedroom window in the middle of the night. Memories of lights flashing off and on, the garage door spring shooting across garage like a misguided rocket, an uninvited visitor lurking in and around the house – those were the negatives. The one positive was having my whole family over to celebrate Christmas, with crackling wood and hot embers in both fireplaces and shadows dancing across the walls. It was a magical evening for me. But moreover, I worked with this house and it gave me strength, independence and confidence in myself. I found I could learn how to do most anything whether it was found in a book, or from the direction of a strong, but gentle voice.

In March of 1998, I found a condominium nearby and wrote a purchase agreement. A bachelor was living there, had barely used the washer and dryer, and was able to move out pretty quickly. I went to two closings on April 7, 1998, saying goodbye to my Wheel Horse tractor, spacious lawn and comfortable home, and then hello to the pretty condo with no lawn to mow and no snow to shovel. My only hesitance was the stairs –stairs up to the bedrooms, stairs down to the basement and my computer and sewing room. There were nights after getting off work following long shifts that my legs just gave out. Totally exhausted, I'd crawl up the stairs on my hands and knees.

I began to relax in my new place. I loved the gas fireplace and the glow it gave the living room and dining area. The off-white carpeting was in nice shape, but the stark white walls just didn't seem to fit, so I called my painter friend, Tim again and he agreed to come over and paint the living room while I was at work.

"So what color are we doing, Beth?"

"The walls should be a deep blue–the color of the night sky approaching dusk."

"You sure you want to go that dark? It'll make the room look smaller."

"That's alright. It's what I need right now."

We settled on a shade of periwinkle blue. People who came to visit would remark that being at my house gave them a sense of tranquility. I felt it, too.

Meanwhile, my sister, Terry had gotten very involved with the church she attended in Clarkston. She had become perseverant in her mission to get me to join her.

"Come on, Beth – just meet me there on Sunday. Then we can go have breakfast afterward."

I was a sucker for breakfast out. I had been missing in action as far as my churchgoing, so I finally agreed to meet her there one Sunday. It was a bit awkward at first, but I slowly became more comfortable returning to my spirituality. It had been a long time—actually since I'd been in my teens that I felt connected to a higher power. My friend, Londa had been largely responsible for that and I never really thought about what had caused me to drift away like I did.

Then in 1999, I had this visitor in the night that so frightened me and caused me to confront my own belief system. It all came to a head and became my "brief encounter" in Chapter One.

EPILOGUE

It took some time before I could truly address the most crucial things concerning me: the directions my life had taken as a whole, my loves, and my experiences gleaned from them all. I recall sitting on a bench in the church lobby after a Sunday morning service trying to explain to my sister what had transpired in my bedroom with my "visitor" in the night the week before, and its impact on me. My brief encounter had so moved me that I could barely speak. And simply put; I realized I had encountered many angels in my life. I was rescued from dogs by a man who just suddenly appeared there for me out of nowhere. My life was spared from drowning at fifteen when I should have drowned. Someone gave me that extraordinary calm when I thought I would die lying in a bathtub. Who was with me and helped me to make my way home several hours after I was raped and dumped like trash into a parked car in the harsh winter? Who watched over me when I was on the hospital gurney awaiting surgery and hoping I'd never wake up? How many strikes to the chest would it have taken to kill me and what made my husband suddenly pass out and release me? Why did it suddenly occur to a photographer to call me on a day that I'd planned to end my life and interrupt me just then?

Now, the bedroom scene I had struggled with seemed so clear to me now. The man's hand that was in front of my face wasn't there to harm me – it was to help me. It was an outstretched hand for me to recognize – a symbol of goodness. This was to be my most powerful angel yet if I would only take its offering. I needed to stay close to God and savor the wonder. I had been there before when I accepted the Lord at age twelve. Then the backsliding continued into my late teens through to my forties. I had prayed many times when I was in trouble during that stretch and needing a rescue of one kind or another, but why then and no other time?

I would go on to explore different directions in nursing like oncology and hospice and see miracles in the making. I knew that attempting to bargain with God was frowned upon, but I believe we came to some form of agreement – I would serve to help heal people if I could remain healthy enough to do it. In the last twenty-two years, my M.S. has never caused me to miss even a day of work to which I'm incredibly grateful. I'm not saying there haven't been uncomfortable moments in my life – there have, but they've been tolerable and I consider myself very blessed. Now, I make it a point to pray nearly every day, sometimes even twice. My prayers are mostly of thanks, and special ones for those dear to me, and for others who I find intolerable and needing a prayer or two. I was baptized for the first and only time at age fifty-two.

My biggest regret was when I realized none of my husbands and I had spent any time together in a spiritual setting unless it was for someone's wedding. We never went as a couple to church. For Ray, Sundays were for golf. With Greg it was for sleeping in after a very late Saturday night at work; with Gil it was just for being lazy, drinking coffee, and reading the Sunday papers. Would these marriages have had a fighting chance if we had shared spiritual intimacy between us? I'll never know.

After the brief encounter I knew that I needed to forgive those who had caused me so much pain in the past – namely important men in my life, good and bad. Carrying the hatred of it all was toxic. I do believe that all of the negative energy can make you sick. It was a long time in coming.

In a symbolic gesture, I wrote out four slips of paper. As I stood at the edge of my lake, I lit each one on fire and let the wind carry it away. Three carried the identical message inside: To Ray: "I forgive you." To Greg: "I forgive you." and to Gil: "I forgive you." The fourth was labeled: "To My Rapist" and inside it said, "You suck."

Well, three out of four isn't bad.